LEVERAGING
YOUR
COMMUNICATION
STYLE

Enhance Relationships,
Build Bridges,
and Reduce Conflict

John Jackson and Lorraine Bossé-Smith

Abingdon Press
Nashville

LEVERAGING YOUR COMMUNICATION STYLE
ENHANCE RELATIONSHIPS, BUILD BRIDGES, AND REDUCE CONFLICT

Copyright © 2008 by John Jackson and Lorraine Bossé-Smith

This book is printed on acid-free paper.

Library of Congress Cataloging-in-Publication Data

Jackson, John, Dr.
    Leveraging your communication style : enhance relationships, build bridges, and reduce conflict / John Jackson and Lorraine Bossé-Smith.
        p. cm.
    Includes bibliographical references.
    ISBN 978-0-687-64751-4 (cloth : alk. paper)
    1. Communication—Religious aspects—Christianity. I. Bossé-Smith, Lorraine, 1966- II. Title.
    BV4597.53.C64J33 2008
    253—dc22

                                                            2008015659

08 09 10 11 12 13 14 15 16 17—10 9 8 7 6 5 4 3 2 1
MANUFACTURED IN THE UNITED STATES OF AMERICA

To our families for loving us even though we move fast, helping us slow down when we need to, and supporting us always.

We hope that we have leveraged our (and your!) communication styles because we love you and want you to know that.

Contents

Acknowledgments

I want to thank all those great communicators I have known in life—whether you were up in front of thousands or just being with your friends and family. Many of these communicators are well-known pastors who have opened their lives and communication skills to me every week. No book is ever the result of a single person, and this book is no exception. Our dear friends at Abingdon are making the process of writing and publishing a real joy. My children (Jennifer, Dena, Rachel, Joshua, and Harrison) and my wife, Pamela, are joy and stability in the midst of any life storm. A special thanks to the staff, Accountability Team, and people of Carson Valley Christian Center, where I have the privilege of serving as Founding Pastor; you make my heart beat fast, and I'm forever thankful for your place in my life!

Dr. John Jackson

Thank you, team Abingdon! You have all been a joy to work with, and I'm so glad we finally got to meet in person at ICRS.

To Johnny Godwin, a dear friend, mentor, and inspiration—you're a "good egg"! I so appreciate your investing in my life, and I thank God for our paths crossing years ago at NHP.

Ask my family, and they will tell you that we certainly aren't perfect. We didn't have this kind of information when we were growing up, but despite "the good, the bad, and the ugly (and the Jimmy)," we *are* family.

To my in-laws, although we come from different tribes, I greatly appreciate your love and support as if I were your own daughter. Thanks, Mom and Dad.

Always to my husband, Steve, who is my greatest cheer-leader and biggest fan—thanks for everything!

—*Lorraine Bossé-Smith*

Can You Hear Me Now?

Where are you from? Mars or Venus? Presumably, we figure it out based on gender, at least according to John Gray in his bestselling book *Men Are from Mars, Women Are from Venus*. But how do I really know where you are coming from: your perspectives, your hopes, your dreams, your pains, and your background? The only way I (John) can know that is if you communicate with me. For us to really communicate, we not only have to talk and listen to each other, we also have to understand what the other means by what he or she says. Ideally, I'll appreciate your perspective and values, and you'll appreciate mine. What starts out appearing to be a simple exercise between two people is often deceptively difficult. Communication in marriage, in relationships, and in the workplace often seems complicated . . . because it is!

Miscommunication often brings about disastrous consequences in personal and professional relationships. Given what is at stake, one might wonder if any hope exists for becoming a better verbal communicator and for understanding more of what others are communicating. Be encouraged because we believe incredible hope is available in this book!

We believe you can become a better communicator and actually leverage your own personal communication style for greater impact. Becoming an excellent communicator will increase your effectiveness in business and personal relationships. We think you can leverage your communication style by becoming a better speaker *and* a better listener.

Over the course of these ten chapters, we will equip you to understand your own communication style and the style of those who are on your team and in your relationship world. Our goal as authors is to give you perspective and helpful tools that will expand your influence and impact. As a pastor and author, I have learned over time that becoming a better listener helps me understand my audiences and relationships better. Once I know the needs of those I am in relationship with and once I know the perspective of my audience, I am better able to serve and lead them as a communicator and author. It is based on our experiences with our relationships and audiences that Lorraine and I share these tools for leveraging your communication style. The materials you read in the next pages will not only describe your style but will also help you understand the respective styles of those you love and work with.

Many of you will want to take the test immediately and then read the chapter that relates to your particular communication style (yes, we know who you are!). Not only is that "allowed," but it may work the best for you. However, we do encourage you to read the other chapters that relate to other styles and topics that affect all of us. Understanding others is important because communication is *never* one way. Communication is *always* a two-way experience. If you speak and I listen but do not understand, then communication has not occurred. If you truly want to leverage your communication style, understanding and appreciating the other styles is an essential part of enhancing the dynamic and complex reality we call communication.

One final thought before we begin the journey together. You might assume that authors who write a book on effective communication are expert communicators. Both Lorraine and I would be the first to admit our shortcomings (well, actually, our respective spouses and team members might be the first to admit to our having communication shortcomings!). We are not "experts" at anything about communication *except* that we each have practiced, studied, and taught communication for over three decades. We long to be effective communicators ourselves and hope to give you a small window into our own souls as you begin the journey yourself. Thanks for joining us in this experience, and as you learn to leverage your communication style, my prayer is that you will be a greater communicator than you would have previously ever dared to dream.

Dr. John Jackson

I don't know how your family taught you to communicate, but mine (Lorraine) taught by observation. I don't think I'm alone here, and I believe most people "catch" how to communicate from their families rather than specifically being instructed on the proper way. Certainly, the school system offers assistance in the areas of sentence structure and formalizing thoughts for speeches, but overall, we are a direct product of our upbringing. *Eeeegads!* That explains a lot! I was basically raised as an only child (my siblings are much older than I), so I didn't have brothers and sisters to learn from or practice on; all I had was my parents. Then I lost my father when I was thirteen, so I was left with only my mother, who held everything inside, God bless her soul. She didn't show emotion, nor would she discuss her feelings. She tended to gunnysack things so that when she finally had enough, she would explode . . . not a super example of communication. But like all of us, I cannot change what I grew up with. As an adult, I have had to learn more effective ways of communicating, and the concepts in this book have been instrumental for me.

I think it is not until we marry that we realize the rest of the world is not like us or our family "tribe." Somehow we go about our business and expect the world to speak like us and to adhere to our tribal rituals. If they do not, we often wonder, "What is wrong with them?" However, when we are intimate with someone 24/7 or work with people day in and day out, we quickly begin to see our own communication deficiencies. What we thought was "the only way" of communicating turns out to be "just one way" of communicating . . . one that works for us but may not work for others. The good news is that our close relationships, whether at work or home, provide us an excellent opportunity to improve our communication skills. In *Leveraging Your Communication Style*, we offer insight into the different communication styles and how you can enhance your relationships by improving your communication skills.

We know you can communicate. You have been communicating since you were a tot because life *is* communication. In fact, even when you are not saying anything, you are sending a message. What John and I want to do is help you first understand yourself and then others, realizing that different people require different methods of communication. Like breathing, we really do not need to think about how to "talk," but rather we need to concentrate on *how* we present what we have to say.

If you do not speak Russian and you are attempting to give directions to a Russian who does not speak English, you can increase the volume of your message all you want, but it still will not be received. If the Russian continues to ask questions in Russian, you will both be very frustrated because neither of you is adapting to the other's language, leaving a huge barrier between you. Likewise, people with different communication styles are essentially speaking different languages. Consider *Leveraging Your Communication Style* your translator. We are here to help you speak different communication styles with ease and confidence!

As a speaker and corporate trainer, I have been brought into many companies across the country to address issues such as time management or team building. About 90 percent of the time, however, the real issue is not what the company contracted me for but instead is a communication breakdown. Leaders come in all shapes and styles (read our book *Leveraging Your Leadership Style* to find out which one you are!), but no matter who they are, they can sometimes get stuck in the philosophy that their staff needs to speak their language. This will lead to a very one-sided relationship, resulting in miscommunication and conflict, which causes frustration and costs money! Everyone benefits from learning to speak the different styles we outline in this book, no matter what your role, position, or title. So get ready for a fun journey of exploring, discovering, and learning, one that will build stronger relationships in your life and reduce conflict. I'm game for that, are you?

Lorraine Bossé-Smith

CHAPTER ONE

The Fine Art of Communication

The real art of conversation is not only to say the right thing in the right place, but to leave unsaid the wrong thing at the tempting moment.

Dorothy Nevill[1]

Winston Churchill is one of the best known speakers in our time, and he had a great impact both as a communicator and as a listener. One time, a rather boring speaker of Parliament was rambling on and on, and Churchill was sitting with his eyes closed. The speaker noticed that Churchill's eyes were closed and asked, "Mr. Churchill, must you sleep while I am talking?" Churchill's response was, with his eyes still closed, "No, it is purely voluntary." Another time, a female member of Parliament was quite upset with him and said, "Mr. Churchill, you make me so mad; if you were my husband, I would put poison in your tea." Churchill's response was "Madam, if you were my wife, I would drink it." Churchill certainly had a way with words![2]

How we communicate—that is, how we talk, listen, understand, and interact with others on our team—determines the influence we have in our relational world. If Lorraine and I have a consistent belief in our previous book, *Leveraging Your Leadership Style*, and this book, *Leveraging Your Communication Style*, it is this: life is about relationships! We think your relationships with God, your spouse, your family, your coworkers, your neighbors, and your friends are the core of life. Communication stands at the center of each of these relationships. This book will help you become a better communicator by equipping you to discover how you can best speak and how you can become a better listener. In the next few pages, you will be introduced to the various aspects of speaking. Then, in the chapters that follow, Lorraine and I will help you (1) discover your own communication style and (2) learn, as both a speaker and a listener, how to interact with others who have different styles of communication.

It Is about Give and Take

It may surprise you to hear that most of us need *much* more help learning how to listen than we do learning how to speak. You probably picked up this book looking for some tools and techniques that will help you become a better speaker, but we would be irresponsible not to also help you become a better listener. The Bible tells us this truth in James 1:19-20: "My dear brothers, take note of this: Everyone should be quick to listen, slow to speak and slow to become angry, for man's anger does not bring about the righteous life that God desires"(NIV). I can't tell you how many times over the course of my life that I have wished I were slow to speak and quick to listen!

So, what is communication all about? At the heart, communication is telling *my* story and listening to *your* story. If I am in the workplace and you are telling me about the sales project, but when you do, a part of you is involved in the story. When I am telling you about what I did last weekend, I am telling you something about me. When we communicate, we are sharing our stories. Artists understand this particularly well because when they sing, paint, write, or dance, they are expressing part of their soul—the deepest part of themselves. When you talk, remember that you are sharing part of yourself with others, and when others are speaking, they are sharing part of themselves with you.

How important is communication in the workplace? It is a *big* issue, and getting *bigger!* For instance, in a 2002 survey of 1,104 employees around the country, 86 percent of the respondents said that their bosses seem to consider themselves great communicators, but only 17 percent said their bosses actually communicate effectively. "We thought there was a communication gap, but it turned out we were totally wrong. It's not a gap; it's a chasm," says Boyd Clarke and Ron Crossland, who include the survey in their book *The Leader's Voice: How Your Communication Can Inspire Action and Get Results!*[3]

Bridging that communication chasm is what this book is all about. Regardless of whether you are communicating with one person, with a small group, or with a large audience, you will need to understand the mechanics of basic communication. The remainder of this chapter will help you understand the basics of effective spoken communication.

Three Keys to Communication

Since we believe that all communication is ultimately about relationship, we urge each person to think of communication in light of facts, feelings, and figures. Facts are the data and details that we are trying either to share or to get agreement on with our audience. Feelings are the emotions we are either experiencing or want our audience to experience. Figures are the symbols or images that help us connect with our audience. We have all experienced speeches or presentations where the speaker appeared to have some level of mastery of the material and seemed genuinely to believe the material had some importance to the speaker and to us. However, we left the presentation feeling frustrated and bored because the presenter never connected with us. I believe that an effective communicator must address three primary engagement targets: the mind (the thinking place), the heart (the feeling place), and the feet (the action place). If the speaker does not do this, then he or she has missed the mark.

Years ago, I (John) was fortunate to have a fantastic experience in a college communications class. I loved the experience so much that I ended up taking two more classes from the same professor. That professor often trained corporate presenters, and I will forever be in debt to him for his excellent training. He was always clear about the importance of connecting at the cognitive (head), affective (heart), and behavioral (feet) levels with the audience. Based on the professor's advice and the advice in Stephen Covey's *Seven Habits of Highly Effective People*, I always try to "begin with the end in mind." In other words, what do I want this person to do, or what difference should this conversation make? By starting from that perspective, I can arrange the three elements (facts, feelings, figures) and the three points of engagement (head, heart, feet) as I outline my presentation.

Facts

Facts are the tangible part of your presentation; they are where you try to connect with the mind of the people in the audience. People are interested in your facts (your information or expertise) if you show that you understand the relationship between your facts and their circumstances. In essence, you are connecting the dots. When you are presenting in a one-on-one conversation or in any group of fewer than ten people, it is very important *not* to have the facts be the primary driver of the communication. When you can see the "whites of their eyes," the primary driver of the communication must come from the heart. People need to know that you care about them and are speaking to them, not assaulting them with a series of facts that may or may not connect with the issues that they are concerned about.

On the other hand, when you are in a larger audience, facts often help to establish credibility. A tried and true framework for speaking comprises the three questions, "What? So what? Now what?" By having mastery of your facts and information with a larger audience, you help establish your credibility. But even here, be careful! Reciting reams of information without relating to your audience at the point of their felt need is a dangerous maneuver (and a potential sale or relationship killer).

Feelings

People don't care about how much you know until they know how much you care.

Feelings are the "soft" part of your presentation; they are where you should try to connect with the hearts of the people in the audience. Many speakers find it easy to dismiss this aspect of communication, as though dismissing it would make it go away. Friends . . . *stop*! *Everyone*, regardless of his or her style, to whom you are speaking has feelings and emotions, and your effectiveness as a communicator is directly related to your ability to connect your story to *his or her* story. However, you must remember that your primary focus in most communication is not simply to make your audience feel something, but for them to take some action. The "heart" part of your presentation must be woven in such a way that you are able to connect the listeners' mind (thinking) and feet (action) through their heart (feeling). Whatever we feel strongly about, we will do. What we only accept in our head will never be lived out in our feet. All behavioral change happens with a thought that begins in the head, gets rooted in the heart, and then gets lived out through the feet.

One particularly effective way to communicate feelings is to be willing to tell your own story and some of how you felt at a certain moment. Since I (John) am a pastor of a large church, I speak to well over a thousand people every week. Part of what people comment about is that I am very "real," and what I take from that is that when I share my story with them, they are able to relate to me at the heart level.

Figures

Figures are where we establish symbols, visuals, paradigms, or values that can help people translate their thoughts and feelings into actions. I know that I personally wrestle with communicating well with figures. Though I don't doubt the old saying, "A picture is worth a thousand words," I find that I personally am so "text" oriented that I have to be very intentional about including "pictures" in my presentations. One of the ways that I have overcome this is to use common images in my stories that everyone can relate to. For example, I was recently speaking about things that "overflow" in our lives. So I used the example of the large industrial trashcan in my family's garage at home and a weekly (sometimes two or three times!) ritual where our trash overflows and I have to perform a task that I call "trash management." I get a stepladder, climb up into the trashcan, and holding on to the garage door rails, I step down on the trash. We all have something that overflows in our lives. What is overflowing in your life, and what can you do to change it if it is the wrong thing? I probably spent three minutes of my thirty-minute presentation telling that story, but I promise you, it was a visual image that stuck in people's minds throughout the week. Provide a visual image that gives people a "hook" to hang their thinking on so that they can begin to develop a plan of action.

The goal of these presentation and engagement points is to develop a simple framework for speaking. Another old framework for speaking is to "tell them what you are going to tell them, tell them, and then tell them what you told them." The goal of most of your communication will be to change a behavior and elicit a response. Go after that result with an emphasis on simplicity. I used to play quite a bit of tennis. My advice to people learning to play tennis is the same as it is to those of us learning to speak well. We should master a few basic principles and then learn to execute them with consistency. Years ago, Chief Justice Oliver Wendell Holmes was reported to have said the following: "I don't give a fig for the simplicity this side of complexity, but I would die for the simplicity on the other side of complexity."[4] Learn the basics of communicating well, then do it. This is the key to leveraging your success as a communicator.

You'll never go wrong if you prepare for speaking by thinking about your audience's head, heart, and, feet. Engage your audience with facts, feelings, and figures. Finally, know what you want them to do in response to your presentation before you say your first word. The rest of this book will help you become an excellent communicator. You'll learn how to leverage your communication style by speaking with excellence and by listening with excellence to the communication styles of those in your life.

.

CHAPTER TWO

Discovering Your Communication Style

If you have anything valuable to contribute to the world, it will come through the expression of your own personality—that single spark of divinity that sets you off and makes you different from every other living creature.

Bruce Barton[1]

I (Lorraine) am told that I was born a social bug. Even as a baby, I wouldn't cry but was content as long as I was the center of everything. When the dinner hour rolled around, I was placed right in the middle of the dining room table for all to see (and pass food around). I would have my own conversation and be happy as a clam. As I grew, I would sing and dance for my parents, putting on plays I created in my head. Once puberty hit, I spent hours on the telephone with friends, the ones I had just seen moments before on the school bus! My mother started singing this song to me: "You talk too much . . . You just talk, talk, talk!"[2] I guess I was destined to be a speaker!

Communication is something we all started doing long before we even said a single word. As little infants, by crying my sibling and I informed our mother and father when we were hungry or needed to be changed. Amazingly, our parents could actually discern one cry from another. We would smile when we were happy and reach out for things we wanted. Without speaking a word, we communicated. As we grew, we learned to replace grunts and gurgles with words. We cried when we were sad or hurt. Since we have all been communicating our entire lives, one would think we would be masters of it, yet the bookstores are full of books on how to get along better with others, reduce conflict, and improve marriages. Why? Talking is easy and communication can seem simple, yet it is actually *very* complex.

The Problem Lies Within

One only needs to read the newspaper or watch the news to see the many challenges our society is facing that are directly connected to communication (or lack thereof). Divorces, lawsuits, and shootings are created, impacted, and resolved through communication. John's chapter, *The Fine Art of Communication*, shares a bit about the importance of communication and what it entails. The act of communication is taught to us, so it is a skill that can be defined. When writing, we have guidelines and rules to follow that have been established and accepted. We even have e-mail etiquette and accepted codes and abbreviations for text messaging today. Communication itself is not the issue, though; *we* are, because each of us is different. Unlike some clothing, "one size *does not* fit all." *People* are what make communication a challenge.

Words are words. How we inflect the words, pace the words, and look as we are saying the words are the true essence of the message. For instance, you can tell your child in a fun, loving, and mischievous way, "Come here, you little monster!" and he or she will giggle and laugh and run toward you. Your child hears the tone and sees your facial expressions. On the other hand, you can yell at your child in an angry, mean voice, "I love you!" and they will probably cry or run away. Your child heard harshness even though the words were kind. In the same vein, the language you choose to speak will either be understood or not. I am not talking about foreign languages here, although a real barrier can exist there too; no, I am suggesting that each of us has our very own distinctive speaking language. This language, or communication style, is the cornerstone of this book.

Different Strokes for Different Folks

I have studied human behavior for many years. I have earned advanced certifications and continually utilize the information on the different personality styles or temperaments in my corporate trainings and books. As I am out speaking, someone always asks if I have heard about the latest, greatest "personality quiz" or "behavior temperament test" and what I think about it. Here's the bottom line: many tools are available to determine your God-given makeup, and they can all have their place. In my opinion, the world is big enough for a variety of methods. However, I do subscribe to a simple way of identifying people's design that is accurate and user-friendly. Some assessments focus on one's thoughts and feelings, which can be great for personal development, but they do not help in understanding the thoughts and feelings of others. Some tests use colors or animals as a way of associating a person's temperament. The list is long, and some of the models and theories can be traced all the way back to the traditions of Egyptian and Mesopotamian civilizations some 5,000 years ago.[3]

Regardless of the method, most everyone agrees that one's childhood can certainly influence one's personality and spirituality. Traumas and any other life-changing events can also affect a person's personality, but who you are today, right now, is our focus. For the purposes of this book, we have created an exclusive assessment that is easy to take, personal, and effective for discovering your unique communication style as well as the style of others. We call it the CAT (Communication Assessment Tool).

A CAT Tale

Before you jump right into the CAT, let me share with you some insights for taking this assessment. (I know some of you are chomping at the bit because of your personality, but pause just a second here if you will. I promise you will get a more accurate reading). The CAT is not designed to be judgmental or to place you in a confining box. It also does not give us the right to label others negatively. Rather, the CAT can help all of us understand ourselves and others better so that we can improve our relationships. If you read the introduction, you know where John and I stand: Life *is* relationships. We are either building bridges or building walls.

The CAT identifies four different communication styles that we all possess, and no one style is better than the other. We are a combination of all four; that is how God made us. You will probably relate to each statement to some degree, but remember, we are looking for what you do *most* of the time because we generally depend upon one of the styles more heavily than the others—we call that our dominant trait. Even when two people share the same top trait, they may still behave or communicate slightly differently since they will have varying degrees of the other styles. We will discuss this later. Suffice it to say that you have a communication style, and we are about to figure out which one it is!

You've Got Style!

I know you value your relationships at work and at home because you picked up this book. In order for you to get the most out of this book, you will want to take the CAT. It should only take five to ten minutes of your time.

Let me reiterate one more time because it is paramount: no

one style is better than any other. The world needs *all* styles, and we each need all of the traits in us to function.

This assessment is basically a snapshot of you today. Do not get stressed over tomorrow. We can all grow and change. In fact, what you are thinking about at the time of this assessment will influence your answers.

So, if you are using this for your personal relationships, think of yourself in terms of "at home." If, on the contrary, you are reading this book for work, then think of yourself "on the job." You can also take this assessment again. In fact, I encourage you to take it in six months to see if you have changed any.

CAT Instructions

Here are some guidelines to taking the CAT:

- **DO** be honest and answer each question as you really are today. Remember, answers are not "right or wrong."
- **DO NOT** answer questions as you would "like to be" or wish you were. This assessment is only as accurate as your honesty.
- **DO** go with your first response or "gut" feeling because it is likely to be the most accurate.
- **DO NOT** spend a lot of time analyzing or thinking about an answer. Circle a response and move on.

Here we go!

OK, are you ready? Go ahead and read the following questions and circle the answer that you feel *best* describes you (take into account either work or home environment):

1. I picked up this book because I
   A. want to be more successful.
   B. want to enjoy my relationships even more.
   C. want to get along better with others.
   D. want to get more information on how to communicate more effectively.

2. I consider myself to be
   A. quiet and supportive of others.
   B. goal-oriented and seek opportunities.
   C. detailed-oriented and factually based.
   D. fun and energetic.

3. My lifestyle could be described as
   A. structured, planned, and organized.
   B. fast and furious!
   C. high energy, social, and exciting!
   D. comfortable, steady, and stable.

4. I prefer my environment (whether at work or home) to be
   A. bright, colorful and engaging.
   B. warm and cozy.
   C. professional.
   D. clean and organized.

5. When shaking someone's hand, I
    A. firmly grip the person's hand and roll my hand on top.
    B. do what is proper and correct for the situation.
    C. shake with zest and enthusiasm.
    D. gently offer my hand under theirs.

6. When given something new to consider, I need
    A. options so that I can choose what works best for me.
    B. space to warm up to the idea and think about what will change.
    C. acceptance of my feelings toward it.
    D. time to process, digest, and analyze before I decide anything.

7. When communicating something difficult, I will
    A. give the facts without much emotion.
    B. get to the bottom line quickly.
    C. procrastinate first and then listen compassionately.
    D. avoid it and then talk through it with some emotion.

8. When someone else is talking, I will usually
    A. ask what the point or bottom line is.
    B. interrupt and participate in the conversation because I have something to add.
    C. listen patiently, allowing them to share their feelings safely without judgment.
    D. pay attention to the details and focus on the accuracy of what they are saying.

9. I would say that my communication style is
    A. detailed, accurate, and correct for the situation.
    B. interactive, animated, and fun.
    C. soft and supportive.
    D. direct and to the point.

10. I relate best with the following person
    A. Dr. Laura
    B. Barbara Bush
    C. Jim Carrey
    D. Al Gore

11. When sharing a story, I typically
    A. let someone else jump in and help tell it.
    B. get to the point quickly with little fluff.
    C. give all the details chronologically and accurately.
    D. use hand gestures, am animated, and may lose track of time.

12. To relax, if given a choice, I would much rather
    A. do crossword puzzles, Sudoku, or computer games.
    B. rest, read, or sleep.
    C. get active!
    D. visit with friends in person or on the phone.

13. When asked to speak in front of a group, I immediately
    A. panic and worry because I hate talking in front of groups.

    B. accept but move on to something else until the day of.

    C. get excited about the stories I will be able to share.

    D. begin to research, outline, and prepare my PowerPoint presentation.

14. When faced with a conflict, I tend to
    A. address it head on but not always with tact.
    B. get emotionally involved and lose sight of the issues.
    C. avoid it at all costs because I hate conflicts of any kind.
    D. stick to the facts and issues at hand after I have had time to think about it.

15. When walking, I normally
    A. move fast as I have places to go and things to do!
    B. plan my route and stick to it.
    C. enjoy the journey, stopping along the way to say hello to people.
    D. take my time because I'm not in a hurry.

16. If I'm the driver for a road trip, I
    A. make sure that all the passengers in the car are having fun!
    B. check with all passengers to make sure they are comfortable and have what they need.
    C. drive from point A to point B as fast as possible with no stops along the way.
    D. plan the trip thoroughly, include rest stops, and estimate our time of arrival.

17. I love
    A. doing things right the first time.
    B. supporting others.
    C. taking on a challenge.
    D. interacting with others.

18. I am comfortable being
    A. logical and analytical.
    B. persuasive and energetic.
    C. assertive and direct.
    D. patient and personable.

19. Especially when I am under stress, others may see me as
    A. inflexible and critical.
    B. unresponsive and indecisive.
    C. disorganized and emotional.
    D. impatient and pushy.

20. I really hate
    A. being rejected.
    B. losing.
    C. change for the sake of change.
    D. being incorrect.

That should not have been too difficult or taken too much time, although you may have struggled on a few. Remember, we are a combination of these traits. We are trying to focus on your prevailing communication mode. If you are not quite sure about your answers, accept them for today. You can always take the assessment again. Right now, let's score your CAT and discover what *your* communication style is.

CAT Scoring

Using the table below, circle the letter that corresponds with each question. Then count up the number of circles in each column and enter the total at the bottom. The column that contains the highest number is your communication profile.

Note: If you have two columns that are the same number, review the brief descriptions below and select the profile you relate with most. You may want to read both of those chapters in order to truly understand your communication style.

Example: If you circled letter "B" in Question #1, then circle letter "B" in the table below. If you circled letter "C" in Question #2, then circle the letter "C," and so forth. In this example, the person would have an Assertive Communication Style. Make sense?

Sample CAT

Q #	Circle Answer			
1	A	(B)	C	D
2	B	D	A	(C)
3	B	C	(D)	A
4	(C)	A	B	D
5	A	C	D	(B)
6	(A)	C	B	D
7	B	(C)	D	A
8	A	B	(C)	D
9	(D)	B	C	A
10	A	(C)	B	D
11	(B)	D	A	C
12	C	D	B	(A)
13	B	(C)	A	D
14	A	B	(C)	D
15	A	C	(D)	B
16	C	A	B	(D)
17	(C)	D	B	A
18	(C)	B	D	A
19	D	(C)	B	A
20	(A)	B	C	D
Total	**7**	**5**	**4**	**4**
CAT Profile	**Assertive**	**Animated**	**Attentive**	**Accurate**

Now *you* do it!

Q #	Circle Answer			
1	A	B	C	D
2	B	D	A	C
3	B	C	D	A
4	C	A	B	D
5	A	C	D	B
6	A	C	B	D
7	B	C	D	A
8	A	B	C	D
9	D	B	C	A
10	A	C	B	D
11	B	D	A	C
12	C	D	B	A
13	B	C	A	D
14	A	B	C	D
15	A	C	D	B
16	C	A	B	D
17	C	D	B	A
18	C	B	D	A
19	D	C	B	A
20	A	B	C	D
Total				
CAT Profile	Assertive	Animated	Attentive	Accurate

Make a note of the highest category and read the brief description below. The next chapter will have more on what this means, and you also have a specific chapter dedicated to your unique communication style! How cool is that?

You're a Cool CAT

Assertive Communication Style. Congratulations! You can speak your mind, easily and directly!

Animated Communication Style. Congratulations! You are a talkative person who is interactive, engaging, and energetic!

Attentive Communication Style. Congratulations! You are a good listener. You wait your turn and are very supportive and compassionate when you speak.

Accurate Communication Style. Congratulations! You are analytical. You focus on details and speak concisely and accurately.

Now let's dig deeper into what each of these styles means so that you can better understand your communication approach and how it affects those in your life. Richer relationships, here you come!

CHAPTER THREE
Understanding Your Communication Style

Sometimes I think that the main obstacle to empathy is our persistent belief that everybody is exactly like us.

John Powell, S. J.[1]

Congratulations! You have just learned what your specific communication style is, and you have received a very brief description of it. You now have a word to associate with your particular approach: Assertive, Animated, Attentive, or Accurate. Each of these words gives you some idea of your personality, but this book does not stop there. We believe that to truly improve your relationships (and life), you must also seek to understand others. The following chapters will provide you with concrete ways to evaluate others' communication styles without judgment.

Before you jump to the chapter dedicated to your style and how best to communicate with others though, you might want to take a look at this chapter because it explains a bit more about how each of the styles fluctuates and moves within us. Remember that we have all of the four temperaments or traits in us at all times; we are simply accessing one more than the others because it is most comfortable.

The CAT Wheel

Let's start off with a visual aid that shows you each of the communication styles in what we call the CAT Wheel.

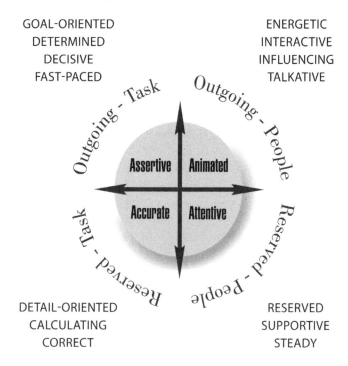

GOAL-ORIENTED
DETERMINED
DECISIVE
FAST-PACED

ENERGETIC
INTERACTIVE
INFLUENCING
TALKATIVE

Outgoing - Task

Outgoing - People

Assertive | **Animated**

Accurate | **Attentive**

Reserved - Task

Reserved - People

DETAIL-ORIENTED
CALCULATING
CORRECT

RESERVED
SUPPORTIVE
STEADY

When you look at the wheel, you will notice that Assertive and Animated communication styles have something in common: they are both outgoing. Yet, Assertive styles are focused more on tasks, which they share with the Accurate communication style. The Accurate approach, however, is more reserved like the Attentive. But the Attentive style is more concerned with people, as is the Animated style. The styles that are next to each other share a common trait, so they can communicate with each other a little easier than can those personalities who do not share a common trait. For instance, Assertive and Attentive communicators are opposite each other. They share nothing in common and must work harder at appreciating the other person's style. This can be done, and we'll show you how. If you ever wanted to learn how to work with a difficult person, keep reading. Chances are, your associate is your opposite.

Each of the communication styles can generally be described in a few words. Look at each of the styles and the associated words. You should find that you relate best with the words in the area that your assessment scored you in. Then again, you may also feel that you connect with a couple of words from another profile. If you do, you are normal and have nothing to worry about. That is the point of this chapter: you are a blend of all the approaches.

Here is how it works for me (Lorraine). My dominant communication style is Assertive. Everything I do is fast. I am goal oriented and very decisive. As much as I enjoy getting things done, though, I also enjoy high-energy activities and being with people and interacting, so I easily move from Assertive to Animated on a regular basis. Even at a young age, I was moving through my blend of styles. I liked being the center of attention, was very talkative, and loved being in charge! Regarding my opposites, I am also very comfortable with details and structure, so I can smoothly transition to the Accurate part of my personality without too much thought. The last place I go is the Attentive side of my makeup. This does not mean I don't support people, but it does mean that I am not very reserved or slow paced. I thrive on variety, and "steady-as-she-goes" is the last place I land. Nonetheless, I do use this part of my personality at the right times.

Each trait has its positive attributes as well as its weaknesses. When we score higher in one style and lower in the others, it does not mean we are deficient; it simply means that we are wired differently. Take a look at my "blend" below and how I process on a regular basis. In fact, this can happen a bazillion times a day!

Lorraine's Personality Panel

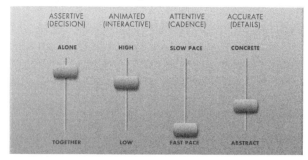

Yes, a bazillion. I am not doing the same thing every minute of every hour, nor am I with the same people, so I am adjusting to fit the situation. That constant change process makes it imperative for us to understand each aspect of our personality. When you know that you can tap into other parts of your personality as needed, you have the ability to speak another person's language and build bridges!

Your Blend

In my years of studying and training others in personality and human behavior, I've concluded that approximately 35 percent of people in the world are Attentive communicators, 30 percent are Accurate communicators, 25 percent are Animated, and 10 percent are Assertive. As I look at this breakdown, I am extremely grateful to God; he knew what he was doing when he made the world a mix of all the styles! Let's picture some scenarios for a moment:

1. If the world were all Assertive types, who would follow all the orders they give? Great thoughts, ideas, and inventions would sit because execution and follow-through are not the strengths of Assertive types.
2. If the world were all Animated types, we would have a blast! Life would be one big party! But alas, not much would get done, and we would probably all starve to death.
3. If the world were all Attentive types, everyone would get along, support each other, and have less stress.

However, nothing would change, and nothing new would be created. No rocking the boat here!

4. If the world were all Accurate types, superb plans would be drawn and impeccable rules and laws would be enacted, but they would never be good enough. No action would be taken, but everything would be neat and tidy!

These are generalizations for fun! I hope you get the picture: the world needs us all! And, we could not function if we did not have each of the traits within us. Yes, God knew what he was doing.

Look back at your assessment; you scored a different number in each of the areas. Chances are that your numbers are not the same as someone else's; thus, even though you may have a similar blend to someone else, you will still execute it in a unique way. The key is to understand what each of these traits means in relation to the others. We are going to spend some time on each of them generally before you proceed to your specific chapter.

Personality Panel

The Personality Panel illustrates the blending of styles a bit more by displaying the unique traits associated with each of the communication styles. You saw my "snapshot" for normal conditions above. I typically make quick decisions and have no problem handling them alone if need be. I am fairly interactive (outgoing) and enjoy a faster pace (cadence).

Depending upon the situation, I can be very detailed or more global. Circumstances are always changing, so I adapt as necessary. I will move my traits up or down accordingly.

Consider your traits like levers on a board. When you need more of one, you raise it; when you need less of another, you lower it. The beauty of this is that you can adapt instantly to meet the needs of the person you are speaking to, on the spot! If you aren't normally detailed-oriented, you can be for a brief moment in time. I like to call it "visiting a trait." You may not want to live in the world of the Accurate profile, but you *can* go there any time you need to get the job done or speak another person's language.

Below is a blank Personality Panel. Taking the information from your CAT and the Blend Wheel, place your lever levels in a place that best represents you *most* of the time. This will give you a good visual image of your traits when you are in your comfort zone. The higher or lower a lever is, the more work it takes you to move it up or down. The closer your lever is to the middle of the graph, the easier it is for you to adapt.

ASSERTIVE (DECISION)	ANIMATED (INTERACTIVE)	ATTENTIVE (CADENCE)	ACCURATE (DETAILS)
ALONE	HIGH	SLOW PACE	CONCRETE
TOGETHER	LOW	FAST PACE	ABSTRACT

Your Personality Panel

Remember my saying that each communication style has its strengths? These strengths when pushed too high can become a weakness. For instance, if I am so independent and decisive that I never ask for help with my major decisions in life, I am likely to make a lot of mistakes. If, on the other hand, I slow down when appropriate to glean the advice of others, I can avoid making some major blunders. It is the same for each of the styles: too much interaction without action leads to chaos; too slow of a pace, and opportunities are lost; and too much of an emphasis on the details, and everything becomes paralyzed by the analysis.

If you have a trait in the higher quadrant, it does not mean that you are a monster. You will just expend more energy moving it down to adjust to the situation. If you are in the lower quadrant of a trait, it does not mean you are a loser. You simply will spend more effort moving it up when required. We all have the ability to adapt and become what we need at the time. Those who truly understand this principle will have richer relationships because they can learn to speak to others and not get stuck in their own style, expecting everyone to cater to them.

Let's look at some of the primary traits of each style, and then you will be ready to move on to your specific chapter!

Assertive Communicators

One of the most dominant traits for the Assertive communicator is the ability to make quick decisions. Every one of us makes decisions every day, but the faster they are made determines the level of the Assertive style in your personality. Again, scoring higher in this area does not mean you trample others callously, and scoring lower does not mean you are indecisive. If you scored lower in the Assertive area, you simply take more time to make decisions and may petition others in the process. One way is not right and another wrong; it is simply what makes us different.

If you scored higher in this area, you feel comfortable making decisions and can handle the pressure of acting alone if you must. Situations will warrant, at times, that you slow down and have others participate in the decision making process. At those times, you would "lower" your Assertive trait.

Assertive communicators are direct, straightforward, and very bottom-line focused. They are movers and shakers! Some Assertive communicators are Jack Welch, Hillary Clinton, Lee Iacoca, and Rudy Giuliani.

Animated Communicators

One of the best ways to describe Animated communicators is in their interaction with others. Each of us interacts with others, but the Animated person is much more energetic and talkative than most. If you rated higher in this category, you are very outgoing and love people. Those who are lower in this area are more reserved and prefer one-on-one settings to large groups.

If you relate with the Animated profile, you are comfortable speaking in front of groups and being the center of attention. You are verbal and usually very inspiring to others simply because you have so much energy. When you must, you can be more quiet and reserved by lowering this trait. Other Animated communicators are Oprah Winfrey, Robin Williams, Bill Cosby, Jim Carrey, and Jay Leno.

Attentive Communicators

One way to spot Attentive communicators is to watch their pace, both in body movement and in speech. If you are an Attentive communicator, then you score higher in the Cadence category because you enjoy taking life a little slower; in fact, you prefer routines and may resist some changes if they appear rash and unnecessary. This does not mean that you cannot hurry up or do things efficiently. You, like the other personality types, can lower this trait to engage in a quicker pace; you just will not want to live there forever!

If you relate with this profile, you are a great listener, often talking much less than those around you. Speaking in front of large groups is not your favorite thing to do—you much prefer to sit down one-on-one and have a quality conversation. When required, you can pick up the pace to speak with the best of them. Other Attentive communicators are Mr.

Rogers, Mother Teresa, Barbara Bush, Jimmy Stewart, and John Maxwell.

Accurate Communicators

You know you are an Accurate communicator when you concentrate on the facts and details of a message more than anything else. If you are an Accurate communicator, you are analytical by nature and process most things chronologically and with great precision. This means that you score higher in the Detail part of the Personality Panel. Often, Accurate communicators feel more comfortable with projects and tasks than they do with people. Does this mean you are all hermits and are socially inept? Heavens, no. You are simply more comfortable dealing with details. When necessary, you will lower the detail part of yourself to enable you to focus more on the person or situation.

Usually quiet and slower paced, you are the one to catch errors others have missed. You have an amazing mind and the ability to foresee challenges and obstacles ahead. Sometimes you can be too critical and will need to increase your interactive trait in order to soften up your message. For Accurate communicators, it's all about being correct. Other Accurate communicators are Al Gore, Diane Sawyer, Sgt. Friday, Ralph Nader, and Jacqueline Kennedy Onassis.

Digging Deeper

I know you are eager to jump into your very own chapter, but hopefully this helped you understand how the styles work. You are not stuck with just one trait; you have access to them all. And that, my friends, is how you can leverage your communication style!

CHAPTER FOUR

Assertive Communicators

We are what we repeatedly do. Excellence, therefore, is not an act, but a habit.

Aristotle[1]

Congratulations! You have an Assertive communication style. Is that a good thing? Is it a "lottery winner"? Are you guaranteed to have effective results as a communicator because you are assertive? Since you are an Assertive, everyone will listen, right? Not so much, but get ready to find out how you can be more successful! One of the reasons we wrote this book is that we believe *everyone* can become a more effective communicator and leverage his or her style in working with others. To do this, you'll have to be intentional about self-awareness, personal mastery, and understanding the communication styles of those you want to reach. Effective communication is *always* a two-way street, and you can't be "one-way" about it, even though as an Assertive communicator, you might like to be!

Who You Are as a Communicator

As an Assertive communicator, you like to have command of your audience, your presentation, and your environment. You generally are well prepared and feel certain of the outcome of any given situation. In fact, the reason you are certain of the outcome is that it is reasonable. After all, if everyone knew what you knew or felt the way you felt, then they would certainly advocate the same position you do, right? Actually, what really happens is that you quickly assess the situation, make your decisions, and are ready to move forward—and then you wonder why everyone else is not on board with you and moving in the same direction. The problem is, they do not make decisions as quickly as you. Have you ever been the first one ready for a family or group outing and ended up "cooling your heels" waiting for everyone else? I'm betting that happens to you on a regular basis—because you are quick and decisive. Rather than see others' slower pace as a deficiency, however, recognize that rapidity is part of *your* unique strength mix. Recognize as well that if you communicate using your primary style without regard to the style of others in the meeting or room, you'll be missing your opportunity to leverage your communication style!

Communication Style

Assertive communicators have to work hard on the relational, people-focused band of the CAT wheel introduced in the previous chapter. For this reason, the key to effective communication for Assertive communicators is to make sure you have an empathic connection with your team members or those in the room whom you are addressing. Because you (and I!) tend to be task-oriented people, we tend to think of effective communication as the accomplishment of a specific assignment. *Stop!* Communicating is *not* an assignment; it is a connection between the communicator and the listener. Particularly as an Assertive person, you must be sure to build a bridge to your audience, regardless of whether your audience is one person or a thousand.

Fear Factor

Deep down inside, Assertive communicators often believe that people they speak with just don't "get it." In fact, many Assertives are so decisive that they often decide quickly that others are not tracking with them and they then shut down their communication efforts. Actually, what people you communicate with must know is that you understand them and are prepared to help them with your expertise and sense of direction without being condescending. You will be far more effective if you learn to read your listeners well (see chapter 8) before barraging them with your facts, your opinions, and the decisions you have already made based on your assessment of the data. Every person sees the world through a set of beliefs and values, sometimes called a paradigm or worldview. The sooner you recognize that you "see" the world around you with a certain set of glasses (yes, we understand that your paradigm or worldview glasses are the "correct" ones!) and that other people wear a different set of glasses, the sooner you will become an effective communicator across the various personality types.

Stress Signals

If you find yourself speaking faster, breathing more quickly, and feeling frustration rising within you as you speak to a team-mate, you are most likely feeling stress as an Assertive communicator. Assertives often have to remind themselves to slow down and calm down. Stress can be reduced if you realize that just as you are acting out of your own sense of certainty about the nature of life (the "paradigm" we talked about earlier), so are others. Because you are likely to have a greater sense of certainty about your subject than any other communication style has, you need to be cautious about overwhelming people with bravado. It is always better to hold some convictions and conclusions "in reserve" until the right moment in your presentation. You will get far more credibility with people if they know that you understand their reality than you will if they just know that you are certain of what you believe.

Communicating with Other Styles

Note that the Assertive and Accurate communicators are focused on details and direction, while the Animated and Attentive communicators are focused on environment and emotions. None of these is exclusively right or wrong, and we all have a little of each in us.

As an Assertive communicator, you can leverage your effectiveness if you become aware of how people "hear" your communication, depending on their style.

Assertive Communicators

Assertive communicators are looking for you to show them respect. But since they are someone with a personality like you, you might think it is a simple matter of speaking plainly just like you would normally do. Think again! When you are speaking with fellow Assertives, you still want to try to understand their values and their decisions. Understanding them will help you communicate with both clarity and sensitivity. Remember, you like to have people communicate respectfully with you, and fellow Assertives will want you to express yourself in ways that demonstrate respect and understanding for their decision-making skills and perspectives.

Animated Communicators

Animated communicators are looking for you to create energy. Animated communicators are animated listeners; they want to sense energy, excitement, and enthusiasm. Just because you are certain of something does not mean they will commit to your course of action or your view of the "facts." The Animated listeners in your audience need to hear your passion and your zeal, or they will not follow you or see it your way. To the extent that you can tell and "sell" a story when you speak rather than focusing on your facts or certainty, you'll become more effective with Animated communicators.

Attentive Communicators

Attentive communicators are looking for you to care about them. In retail sales, the concept is known as "mass customization." My product has to be saleable to the masses, but each customer has to believe I've made the product just for him or her. Attentive listeners in your team want to know that you feel their pain, that you understand their reality, and that you care about them. Even if you're talking business, it is personal to them. Recall Tom Hanks and Meg Ryan in the movie *You've Got Mail.* Even when their characters were trying to be nice to one another, their conversations would dissolve into conflict because Tom Hanks' character—an Assertive type—failed to adapt to Meg Ryan's Attentive style. "It wasn't personal—it was business," he tells her, thinking that will help the situation. "I'm so sick of that!" she replies. "It was personal to *me!*" When you are speaking and connecting with Attentive people, you must find a way to connect at a very personal level. When you are able to connect your personal heartbeat to the heartbeat of your Attentive listeners, you will be an effective communicator with them.

Accurate Communicators

Accurate communicators are looking for you to be Assertive *and* correct: assertive because they have come to expect that from you and correct because that is what they need. You can depend upon Accurate communicators to listen for whether you have accurate information and have verified your sources and your details. Accurate listeners will be less likely to follow you if you play "fast and loose" with statistics and information. Accurate listeners want to know that you have done your research and that you are prepared to defend your interpretation of the data. If you want to win over Accurate communicators, you will need to develop a clear framework upon which to establish both what the truth is and how your information and details are relevant to their circumstances.

Think about the people on your primary work group or team. As you think about each of them, take an initial overview of them and then begin to think about how you interact with them on a regular basis. Use this "cheat sheet" that we have developed in order to record your observations and to document your hunches about each member of the team or group you are working with in order to determine his or her communication style. Don't worry about this seeming overly complex; it is our experience that as you do this with greater frequency it will become second nature to you!

As an Assertive communicator, you will find it helpful to continually develop your capacity *both* as a lifelong learner and as an observer of yourself and others. The more you know about the "what" you are communicating, the better prepared you will feel. The more you know about the "who" you are communicating with, the more effective you will be. Watch other people who communicate well and are the same style as you. What do they do well? How do they present material differently than you do? Watch people who are competent communicators and have a different style than you do. What do they do that is particularly effective, and how is that different from the way you go about the task? You can and will become an effective *and* Assertive communicator!

Communication Cheat Sheet

You have learned about the different styles and how best to communicate with them. How about putting it into practice? Below is a grid for your colleagues or family members. Write their names and fill in your communication tips so that you can have it handy when interacting with these people. This way, you can have stronger, healthier relationships and less conflict.

Communication Cheat Sheet				
Name	Key Words	Tone of Voice	Pace of Speech	Body Language
Person #1				
Person #2				
Person #3				
Person #4				
Person #5				

Assertive communicators like to win, and the best way to ensure that win is to leverage your Assertive communication style. And we know you will do this because you are a doer!

Ultimately, every one of the styles wants to arrive at the same destination. They want to believe, do, or feel the right things, but other people make decisions and undertake directions in an entirely different fashion from you, the Assertive communicator. Regardless of whether your presentation is informative or persuasive, you can work with each type. Here is the likely reality for each of the communication types when it comes to decision making:

- *The Assertive communicator* wants to make sure he or she moves fast and forward.
- *The Animated communicator* wants to make sure everyone else has the same level of excitement.
- *The Attentive communicator* wants to make sure that everyone else is feeling good about the decision or circumstances.
- *The Accurate communicator* wants to make sure that all the details are accurate before committing to a course of action.

CHAPTER FIVE

Animated Communicators

At the heart of personality is the need to feel a sense of being loveable without having to qualify for that acceptance.
Maurice Wagner[1]

I (Lorraine) just watched *The Chronicles of Narnia: The Lion, the Witch and the Wardrobe* again. This classic story of four children sent away from their London home during World War II so they would be safe chronicles the adventures they have while living with an aloof professor. In addition to imparting a powerful message, C. S. Lewis certainly shows that he understood the different personality types because each main character represented a different style. Peter, the older brother, is a classic Attentive sort who is constantly worrying about what he should do for the sake of others. He goes beyond the big brother role to look after each and every person he encounters; thus he turns out to be a great leader in the end. His younger brother, Edmund, on the other hand, is strong willed, defiant, and aggressive. As an Assertive type, he wants what he wants when he wants it or even faster if possible. Edmund gets into some serious trouble and learns some hard lessons. The oldest sister is Susan. She comes across as very negative at times during the film, but the reality is that she is a hard-core Accurate individual who sees the obstacles ahead. Her detailed nature seeks order, reason, and structure. The entire adventure stretches her very existence, and you can see her develop and grow through each ordeal she faces. The youngest sister is Lucy. Lucy is the one who discovers the magical wardrobe first, and her creative imagination allows her to absorb all the wonders of Narnia. After being in Narnia only a couple of minutes, she makes friends with a faun! She loves to play games, giggle, talk, and have fun despite the frightening circumstances. She is the ultimate optimist and thinks the best of everyone. If you haven't seen the movie or read the book, I encourage you to, and I'll bet you will connect best with Lucy because she is an Animated person—just like you.

Who You Are as a Communicator

I assume that you took the assessment in chapter 2 and have determined your unique communication style to be Animated. How wonderful! Animated people are very creative and high energy. You love people! What's the saying, "There are no strangers . . . only friends you haven't met yet"? Animated communicators believe this to be true and live it out. You are not strangers with anyone for long, and you enjoy conversations, socializing, and having fun. You are indeed outgoing, people-oriented folks who interact well and thrive on change, variety, and a faster pace.

Communication Style

The Animated communication style is very informal. You don't want to spend energy on formalities like waiting your turn to talk! No, you want to jump right in! Your mind races a million miles a minute, and you can talk just about as fast when you are excited. And speaking of talking, you have a lot of words to use up in a day. My husband is even higher in this area than I am. On a road trip one year, he literally shared stories, thoughts, and concepts "to" me for over three hours before I finally nudged my way in and said, "Whoa! My ears are swollen, and I can't take in another word!" He was astonished. In his mind, *we* had been talking for hours, but he had failed to notice that I could not get a word in edgewise. He was on a roll!

Animated communicators do have a problem with listening at times. You are so eager to share what is on your mind that you are thinking of what you will say next rather than the words being spoken. You can miss details. I love the Tidy Cats Crystals Blend ad that came out years ago. It pictured four cats staring at a litter box. The Assertive cat, clearly the leader of the pack, with his stern face, asks of the other cats, "Have you been using the litter box or the plant? And *don't* lie to me!" The sweet Attentive cat, peering up with adoring, faithful eyes at the Assertive cat, answers, "The litter box, we promise." The Accurate cat, concentrating deeply on the litter box itself, replies, "The odor-trapping crystals in our Tidy Cats Crystals Blend work really good." Last but not least, the

Animated cat, with a deer-in-the-headlights look and ears back in confusion, mumbles, "We're not supposed to use the plant?" I laugh every time I look at this ad![2] That poor cat missed that part, probably because he was chasing a butterfly or doing something else really cool and fun!

Ever see the Austin Powers movies? "Yeah, baby!" They are pretty silly, but you have to laugh sometimes at what comes out of Austin Powers's mouth—like the scene of the guy with a huge mole on his face. Austin tells himself, "Don't stare at the mole." When he opens his mouth to speak, he says, "Hello, Mr. Mole!" He truly speaks before he thinks, loves a great party (isn't life just one big party?), and never seems to get down, despite life-threatening situations.

As an Animated communicator, you enjoy using your body to assist with your message, and you may find yourself waving your arms around even while talking on the phone! You are very expressive with your eyes and mouth as a way to support the tone you wish. You prefer a high degree of contact with other people. You are not the type of folks to hide away in a cubicle somewhere without any human contact. You would wilt like a flower without water.

Because you are creative, you appreciate freedom to express yourself in a variety of ways. You typically are not a traditionalist, and you like to think outside of the box . . . or in some cases, ask, "What box?" You are fast paced and can be a bit disorganized. As a friend of mine says to me, "Neatness is not on her list." Unless you find organizing things fun, you probably do not put it high on your list, either. Animated people are interactive and engaging, so projects can be cumbersome to you. Words to describe you are often "inspiring," "influencing," "impulsive," "interesting," "impressive," and "illogical."

Fear Factor

A couple of those descriptors may be a little hard to swallow, but remember, we all have areas that, when pushed to the extreme, can cause us to become our own worst enemy. I like to say that the enemy really does lie within. We open our mouth, and it can rear its ugly head! For the Animated individual, what goes up will usually come down. You are so high energy that, when you finally stop, you can often crash and burn. Animated communicators typically have two gears: *full speed ahead* and *stop*! Because you long to fit in and be accepted, you can sometimes be overly sensitive to criticism.

As an Animated communicator, you fear rejection more than anything else because one of your primary needs is to feel loved, accepted, and praised. Forget statistics telling us that people would rather die than speak in front of a group—not with Animated folks. You have no problem getting up in front of a group and speaking, but it is rejection that you fear, and that may very well keep you away, depending upon your level of self-esteem. Animated folks also fear loss of social recognition or connection.

Stress Signals

Again, we all have fears and parts of our personality that, when pushed too far, can become ugly. I love the shirt I have seen that says, "Hand over the chocolate, and nobody will get hurt!" We all need to be watching for the early warning signs. For Animated styles, keeping emotions under control is key. When you are under extreme stress, emotions can run high and start to influence how you come across to others. During times of stress or fatigue, you can be too verbal and can express thoughts inappropriately. In an attempt to dull the pain from a stressful situation, you may simply follow popular opinion, potentially sacrificing what really matters to you. Emotional outbursts can certainly cloud your judgment and may lead to more rejection—the very thing you want to avoid.

Knowing in advance that, as an Animated communicator, you may become too talkative during stressful times can help you address your concerns and needs as they arise instead of letting them build. Be sure to share what is on your mind and in your heart with "safe" people. Not everyone is the right person to confide in. Find someone who is mature and trustworthy, then spend time with him or her alone so you can talk through things that are bothering you. Set your confidant up for success by letting him or her know you just need to vent. This is especially important for male confidants because they need to know that their role is simply to be a good listener. If they know they are not expected to fix anything, they can give you their full attention. But if you do not inform them on the front end, you will both be frustrated. They will keep interrupting you with solutions, and you will want to give up. A little communication will go a long way.

Secrets for Effectively Communicating with Others

Speaking of communication, here is where we set *you* up for success. Understanding your own style is just the beginning. Now it is time for you to focus on how you can communicate to other styles and build those bridges and improve your relationships. Life is all about relationships. You might want to go back and reread some of the descriptions of the other communication styles and start to identify those you work with and live with because now we will give you tips on how to communicate more effectively with them.

Assertive Communicators

Assertive communicators are the people in your life who are to-the-point, goal oriented, and fast paced like you, but they direct their energies towards tasks, not people. Being outgoing and loving people, you can create an immediate wall with these folks by talking too much. One of my clients had a very Assertive communicator as a boss. His boss would actually stand up and walk out on my client when he was speaking because this boss could not be bothered with all those words! This can appear rude; however, when you seek to understand where an Assertive communicator is coming from, you learn not to judge but simply to acknowledge the differences between the two styles.

A better approach to these decisive folks is to give them the bottom line. Rather than telling the supporting story or providing the details, give them the conclusion first. Then, ask them if they would like to hear more. When they say yes, you will have their undivided attention because they chose to listen. It is not that Assertive types cannot listen, because they can, but they must feel in control. Throwing a bunch of words at them that they did not ask for will just frustrate them. Here is a tool for you. Any time you have determined that you are speaking with an Assertive person, imagine that person holding an enormous whiteboard that prevents you from seeing him or her. On the whiteboard are the words "What is in it for me?" Until you answer that question, the whiteboard remains, and you never really get up close and personal. If, on the other hand, you address that concern head on, the words are erased, and the board comes down. That person is now interacting with you, which you like. Everyone wins!

Assertive people get a bad rap because they can come across as pushy and demanding. Remember, we are all made to be different and no one style is better than the other. Seeking to see the world through their eyes helps you realize that they are just doing what they know. They are not trying to do anything to you; rather; they are being who they are made to be.

Pick up your pace, get to the point, and avoid becoming emotional with Assertive communicators, and you will enhance these relationships that once felt strained or difficult. Assertive people can be fun. You just have to allow them to take the lead.

Animated Communicators

These are your friends! You will be at ease with others like you because you communicate in the same way. You all enjoy a fun story, being friendly, laughing, and just having a good time. You really will not need to adapt to blend with other Animated people, but you will want to ensure that you do address the business at hand at some point. Two high-energy people can certainly get off task and lose track of time. I have observed that sometimes everyone can talk at the same time, stepping over each other. But Animated people do not seem to mind; they just talk louder and keep on going! A group of Animated folks can certainly be loud. As a speaker, I love having these people in the audience because they laugh at my jokes. Thank you! Remember, however, that others around you might not appreciate the noise. Be mindful of your surroundings when together with other Animated communicators.

You are naturally informal, animated, and optimistic. Keep it up. You can share as many details as you want, but remember, Animateds may not remember everything specifically. The saying, "Facts tell but stories sell" really hits home for Animated communicators.

Attentive Communicators

People you encounter who are softer and quieter than you but still lean towards people rather than tasks are the Attentive communicators. They are much slower paced than you and prefer more of a one-on-one conversation rather than a group gab session. One of the challenges you will have when speaking to Attentive communicators is slowing down long enough to allow them to talk. If you keep talking, they will patiently wait their turn; however, if you keep going, they may never get a word in edgewise. I like to use the word "pause" because it does not sound so painful. Pausing is temporary. By pausing after you speak, you give them the opportunity to respond. Fight the urge to fill the silence up with more words, but rather concentrate on their body language and eye contact. Once they do speak, do not jump right in over them; instead, listen and acknowledge by nodding or smiling to let them know that you hear them. By leaning in toward them, you can show that you care. Because they are not as high-energy as you, use a gentle tone. Attentive people are very relational, so you will get along well if you show a little patience with them.

Accurate Communicators

If you happen to have anyone in your life whom you feel estranged from or cannot relate with, chances are he or she very well may be your complete opposite, an Accurate communicator. You share something with the other types, but with the Accurate style, you do not have anything in common. They prefer tasks, and you like people. They are reserved, and you are outgoing. They are slower paced, and you are faster paced. This means that it requires more work for you to speak with them. But because you are reading this book, you will have a much easier time!

Remember the white board in front of the Assertive person? Accurate people are holding one up as well, but theirs says, "How?" They are analytical beings. Their brains break every thing down and want to know *how* things work. If you can answer this question for them on the front end, they will receive your message. If you simply share a story or tell a joke, they may not respond. I was once interviewed by a man who had a stone face the entire time. Not once did he break a smile. He went from question to question and showed no emotion. At the conclusion of my interview, I had no idea if he liked me or not. When I got the job, I assumed I must have passed the test. Once I got to know the gentleman, he warmed up, and we got along just fine. He was obviously an Accurate communicator.

You have to earn your way into an Accurate person's world. You do that by being logical, consistent, and detail oriented—all of which can be difficult for you. Again, slow down your pace and focus more on the facts. Do not rush Accurate communicators or push them into a reply. They may need additional time to get back to you on something; give it to them. If you stick to business and remove emotion from your conversation with them, you'll make great strides. Once they feel comfortable with you, you can then laugh and joke around. It is not that they do not have a sense of humor; they can be quite funny. They will want to be funny at the proper time. If you are a stranger, then they will not feel joking is appropriate. Enjoy the process of getting to know them by asking questions and giving information they need in order to get to know you. It will take a little longer than with your Animated counterparts, who are instant friends, but you will have a solid relationship in the end. We could all use more of those.

Communication Cheat Sheet

You have learned about the different styles and how best to communicate with them. How about putting it into practice? On the opposite page is a grid for your family or your team at work. List their names and fill in your communication tips so that you can have this information handy when interacting with them. That way, you can have stronger, healthier relationships and less conflict.

Communication Cheat Sheet				
Name	Key Words	Tone of Voice	Pace of Speech	Body Language
Person #1				
Person #2				
Person #3				
Person #4				
Person #5				

Now go and leverage your Animated communication style!

CHAPTER SIX
Attentive Communicators

Human beings, like plants, grow in the soil of acceptance, not in the atmosphere of rejection.

John Powell[1]

So, you are an Attentive communicator. That means that you probably are paying attention when people speak, right? You really care what the person is saying—and maybe more importantly, what they are feeling while they are talking to you, right? In fact, you have wondered if a story or illustration that someone shared came out of personal pain or joy, right? If so, you are most certainly an Attentive communicator. Attentive people are very aware of the *person* they are communicating with, not just the words they are hearing. Behind every word and around every tone is a feeling, and Attentive communicators want to make sure they hear the personal pain or joy in every sentence. If that sounds like you, then I want you to know how much those of us with other communication styles appreciate you!

Who You Are as a Communicator

Attentive communicators generally help the people they are talking with feel accepted and comfortable; it is actually a gift you have that others have to work on. Attentive communicators intuitively read facial expressions and seek to understand and appreciate the perspective of the person on the other side of the conversation. You are engaged at a personal level with the individual(s) in the room. This is almost always a good thing, unless you happen to be dealing with an Assertive or Accurate communicator! Assertive and Accurate communicators will probably struggle with your personal attention toward them, but you will help them over time. We will get to that later, but suffice it to say that Attentive communicators want to connect with the *person* they are speaking to, not the information or even the passion if it does not directly relate to the person.

Attentive communicators are at the peak of their game when they are in relationship mode. You are at the high relationship end of the CAT personality panel. You want people to have a personal and empathic connection with you, and you want to have one with them! That means that your communication is generally filled with very personal sharing, through which you are inviting your listener(s) to experience your world and to feel what you feel. That passion in you (to connect empathically with those you communicate with) is a powerful force. The challenge for you as an Attentive individual is to realize that everyone else does not always share your passion equally. The more that you can read about and internalize the other communication styles, the better equipped you will be for leveraging your own communication style and effectiveness.

Communication Style

Typically, Attentive communicators will talk more slowly and have definitive gestures that are part of the speaking process. Most Attentive people, particularly in a selling situation, will resist a rush to a decision or judgment. In fact, you often will prefer to move far more slowly than any of the other three types, including the Accurate types, who are always looking to confirm their information and facts; but your primary concern is always the people in the equation, not the information, decision, or excitement. Because of these things, you will often find your fellow Attentive communicators being far more willing to listen than the other types. However, do not assume that their willingness to listen means that they are in agreement with you. In fact, Attentive (similar to Accurate) communicators are listening with strong intent. As opposed to the Accurate communicator who is listening for information, the Attentive communicator's listening is all about the personal factor, asking, *Do I trust and connect with the person who is communicating with me?*

Fear and Stress Factors

As an Attentive individual, you know what paralyzes you. Every communication style has some trigger event or personality type that can become a source of great fear and potential pain. Your primary focus is on people, and you want to know that people feel safe, that they feel valued, and that you are making a heart connection with them. Because of all this, you can sometimes be in a place of fear if you are unable to "read" or connect with the person(s) you are speaking with. You do not like conflict and will avoid it at any cost. When communicating with the other styles, if you do not know what you are up against, you could be in for a conflict right off the bat. What that typically means is that people who are Assertive or Animated will pose the greatest level of discomfort for you. We'll spend some time later on addressing how to communicate with these types, but for now, let's talk about you. How do you handle the surge of doubt and uncertainty that comes when you cannot connect with the person you are speaking with?

Attentive communicators can do several things to conquer their bad experiences and fears of not connecting. Rather than withdrawing and beginning to shut down, which would be your normal reaction, I (John) would encourage you to remember whom you are speaking with. If you are speaking with Assertive or Animated communicators, remember that they are focused on specific goals and experiences. If you can adjust your questions and communications to connect with their focus, you should be able to experience a shift where you can sense an increase in their excitement and passions. Second, determine where the immediate common ground is between you, and build from there. If you can start with agreement on an issue or a decision, you can more easily navigate the course to the greater and more uncertain territory. Finally, if all else fails, pray! I'm only partially kidding. It has been my experience that prayer helps to calm my mind and stabilize my racing heart and restore me to a sense of peace. A peace-filled person will always have an easier time communicating and connecting with others. We cannot have both peace and fear at the same time, so I encourage you to choose peace. I promise you, even Assertive communicators can sense when someone is highly stressed and not at peace!

Communicating with Other Styles

Of all the communication styles, your style has perhaps best positioned you to care about how you connect with the other styles. Since you are attentive already, you probably already sense when other people are just not like you. So, we are going to equip you in this chapter to communicate effectively with those who have other styles. As we review each style, keep in mind that knowing your own style is only part of the journey; understanding and connecting your style to others is what really pays off. Think of this exercise as building a bridge across a river in order to join a group of people building a bridge on the other side. Both groups start on opposing sides of the river, but they have to meet in the middle in order to make the bridge crossable. You are getting ready to cross a bridge that you will build by being attentive to how others communicate. You can do this, and you will be excellent at this task!

Assertive Communicators

As an Attentive communicator, your most difficult communication type will be your Assertive communicator friends because they are your opposite. So, how do you speak and listen well to an Assertive communicator? Let me start with an old saying, "First things first." If you can remember that, you are well on your way to leveraging your communication with Assertive individuals. Assertive people are driven by a vision of the future, and they are result oriented. So what they really want to know is the answer to this question: "Why does this matter to me?" Assertive people are glad you care about them and glad you want to connect with them, but they simply are more focused on *where* they are going than *who* is going with them. So to be successful with Assertive communicators, be sure to start out with why your topic or focus is important— to them! Then (and only then!) can you use your tremendous ability to read their facial expressions and understand their reactions in order to know how much more to share.

When you are listening to Assertive communicators, you will want to focus on the purpose for their communication while you are focused on their person as well. If you can "read" their purpose as well as you read their person, then you can understand their priorities and values. Assertive communicators really do care about other people, and they care about you. However, their "hard wiring" is all about future direction, focus, purpose, and movement. Knowing how Assertives are wired equips you to connect with them at more than one level. Learn to grasp their purpose, and you will be well on the way to leveraging your communication with others who have your most difficult type of communication style.

Animated Communicators

Communicating with Animated people will keep you busy! Animated communicators are expressive, fast talking, and love to keep the interaction going. You will quickly be drawn into the conversation by their engaging personality. Communicating with Animated communicators requires that you establish a personal rapport with them based on *their* "story." So, your first job when communicating with Animated individuals is to figure out what key value, experience, concern, or challenge they are currently facing. Their communication patterns will revolve around that key component. Once you find the key component, you will do great if you can aim your communication toward the heart of that component. If you help your Animated team members or friends realize that you understand their core issue or concern by the way you speak and listen, you will be miles ahead!

Speaking with Animated people will only be slightly difficult for you because you share their focus on people. Because they are faster paced, however, Animated communicators want to see *energy*. So, as a highly relational and deeply caring person, your task as an Attentive communicator is to translate your caring into energy. Animated communicators tend to read hand motions, facial gestures, pace, and tone just like you read eyes. So when you are speaking with Animated communicators, you may have to put a little more energy into being expressive verbally, tonally, and with your hands. Communicate excitement and passion, and you will have the Animated communicators connecting with you at the deepest level. If you find that Animated communicators are interrupting you frequently, you have succeeded in building rapport! This means they are enjoying their conversation with you and are engaged. Everyone has won!

Attentive Communicators

So now you get to communicate with fellow Attentive people. You are right that it will go smoothly for you, but you will have one problem: each of you will be so focused on the other person that you will want to listen instead of talk! The best framework for communicating with fellow Attentive folks is to ensure that you have a direction (agenda) for the conversation, or else you may spend the majority of your time on personal matters that do not relate to your work objectives. Sorry about that, but work objectives matter, and, yes,

I know that I am saying that as an Assertive, but I think you will agree that your team will be happier and more personally fulfilled if you are making corporate and personal progress toward your shared goals. When you communicate with fellow Attentives, be sure to focus both on their personal values and priorities, which comes naturally to you, and on their role in the family, on the team, or in the workplace.

Accurate Communicators

Speaking with Accurate communicators will also not be too hard for you because you share their reserved nature and slower pace. What will be imperative is that you take the time to ensure not only that you concern yourself with expressing personal care for them, which is important to you but far less important to them, but also that you are equally concerned with the details of your facts and figures. The more time you can spend in advance understanding the specific details of your project or proposal and gathering the right information and data, the better prepared you are to speak with Accurate folks. For the Accurate, someone who is sloppy with details is not to be trusted. You can overcome that by paying attention to details. If you do so, the Attentive communicator will hear you loud and clear.

Listening to an Accurate communicator will only be painful to you if you fail to realize that underneath all that precision is a person! Recognize that, as Accurate communicators are citing statistics and future projections, they are really telling you about what is important to them, and it is *not* the numbers themselves. It is the precision and care with which details are handled. Most Accurate communicators care deeply and passionately about the way things are done. You have, therefore, an immediate connection with them that you may not be aware of. You care deeply about the people; they care deeply about the process. Both are indicators of value, and your ability to recognize that they are people of passion will put you miles ahead in the communication process. If you focus on the person behind the details and if you value *both* the person and the precision, then you will make a great connection with the Accurate communicators in your life.

Communication Cheat Sheet

You have learned about the different styles and how best to communicate with them. How about putting it into practice? Below is a grid for your colleagues or family members. Write their names and fill in your communication tips so that you can have this information handy when interacting with these people. That way, you can have stronger, healthier relationships and less conflict.

Communication Cheat Sheet				
Name	Key Words	Tone of Voice	Pace of Speech	Body Language
Person #1				
Person #2				
Person #3				
Person #4				
Person #5				

Because you are Attentive, you will want to know this: I enjoyed writing this chapter about you—thank you for the gift you are to the rest of us!

CHAPTER SEVEN

Accurate Communicators

A manager's personal style—how good he or she is at exchanging information—contributes more to a department's efficiency than the results of any structured or organizational brilliance.
Mark H. McCormack[1]

I (Lorraine) have a friend who has read every single one of my books, front to back. That makes him a very good friend, in my opinion! He is an architect and loves details. In fact, he will usually be the one to find an error, if any, in my writings. He doesn't just read my books, though; he will also seek clarification on anything that doesn't make 100 percent sense, gather more information in areas that he is interested in, and express his thoughts regarding whether he is in agreement with me or not. This logical process makes him ideal for his occupation, and I appreciate his feedback because I know he has really studied my work. As a writer, you often wonder if anyone has read your book. So with my friend, I know at least one person on this earth has read my book. Thanks, Glen!

Since you are an Accurate person too, I know that you have read everything leading up to this point so that you would not miss anything. I have great confidence that you took the assessment and carefully considered each and every question. You certainly will get much more out of this book than those who may have skipped some chapters. Oh, they may eventually go back and review them, and that is okay; but you are obtaining the entire picture now. Bravo!

Who You Are as a Communicator

Accurate communicators are indeed detail oriented. You typically will share a story or experience from the very beginning all the way to the end, not missing a single detail. Your brains work in very chronological and methodical ways. You are analytical and consistent in what you do and say. Being slower paced and more reserved, you can come across as inflexible or critical at times. Your primary concern is to be correct and provide quality answers. Without Accurate individuals, we would not be enjoying many of the fantastic comforts and conveniences of our day. Even if an Assertive or Animated genius came up with the idea, somewhere along the line, an Accurate mind helped put the plans on paper. And details do matter. Look at these alarming statistics:[2]

- Two million documents will be lost by the IRS this year,
- 811,000 faulty rolls of 35 mm film will be loaded this year,

- 22,000 checks will be deducted from the wrong bank accounts in the next 60 minutes,
- 1,314 phone calls will be misplaced by telecommunication services every minute,
- 12 babies will be given to the wrong parents each day,
- 14,208 defective personal computers will be shipped this year, and
- 103,260 income tax returns will be processed incorrectly this year.

Accurate folks are extremely gifted in strategy—thinking down the road. You can see obstacles and hurdles that others cannot (or do not want to) see. We need Accurates in our lives and on our teams. We all have some of this element in us; otherwise, we could not get anything done properly. But those who thrive in this style truly shine when it comes to organizing details, creating structures, and establishing procedures.

Communication Style

When it comes to communicating, Accurate communicators are logical and very businesslike. Whether it is one-on-one or to a group, you will share your message in a precise manner. Accurate presenters often use electronic slideshows to disseminate data efficiently. You usually approach things and people with caution, and you are contemplative, structured, and conscientious.

Accurate communicators are not touchy-feely naturally, so

you usually do not show your emotions. Unlike Animated communicators who can sometimes wear their emotions on their sleeves, Accurate communicators keep everything close to the vest—at least until you know and trust your audience better.

One of my key accounts for a client was an extreme case. Previous attempts had been made by salespeople to "break through" and warm this guy up, but no one succeeded in getting an order. I showed up with a binder full of facts, figures, details, and information pertaining to the product and pointed out some key issues, concerns, and features. I then suggested that he review it at his convenience. I made my recommendations as to which products I thought would fit his needs and niche market, but I deferred to his judgment and said I looked forward to working with him. And at that, I was done with my appointment. I noticed a few family pictures and asked about them, and we began to talk. I shared a bit about me, and by the time I left, he smiled as he shook my hand. I got a nice order a week later. I did not rush him or presume to know his needs better than he. I simply presented as much material as I had and gave him time to ponder, reflect, and decide. For the Accurate communicator, slowing down and allowing time to process is essential. As an Accurate, you do not like to be pushed, rushed, or forced into making a decision until you are ready.

Fear Factor

Now, like all the other styles, some traits can be negative when pushed too far. It is acceptable to take some time to consider whether you will take action, but it is not okay to dig your heels in, refuse to budge, and not select a course of action. For the Accurate communicator, overanalyzing things can literally be paralyzing. Why? Because your greatest fear is being wrong, incorrect, or making a mistake. In order to prevent that, Accurate communicators will thoroughly research and investigate everything. This isn't a bad thing until it gets out of hand and goes on for too long. When it does, other people see Accurate people as very picky, fussy, and difficult.

I spoke with a lady after my speaking engagement on fitness based upon personality style (see my book, *Finally FIT*). She said that she had been researching the right workout program for over two years. She got so caught up in worrying that she would make a mistake, buy the wrong piece of equipment, or join a gym that she did not like that she did not do anything . . . for two years! Meanwhile, she got more out of shape and her health declined. She realized after my talk that she needed to take action. For the Accurate mind, information gathering is fun. But, it can be a trap for you. With the invention of the Internet, the world has been opened up to us. We have much more information available to us now than ten years ago. Just remember this: gathering information is not doing. Sometimes you can get stuck in the "paralysis of analysis." You can read and know everything, but actually doing something is what counts.

Stress Signals

If you find yourself stuck, you might be under too much stress. When Accurate communicators are faced with irrational people, disorder, or antagonistic environments, you will withdraw to what is safe for you: facts, figures, numbers, and so on. We all have those sides of our personality that can be maladaptive, but if we can look for warning signs, we can minimize the negative effects.

When things are moving too fast and everything is changing, give yourself time for cognitive activities. Activities that you can start and finish give you a sense of order and control. Be aware that what you think is simply a factual statement may be critical to someone else. You know that saying, "If you don't have something nice to say, then don't say anything at all?" Take it to heart. The book of Proverbs echoes that same wisdom: "When words are many, sin is not absent, but he who holds his tongue is wise" (Proverbs 10:19 NIV).

One of the biggest complaints from your Assertive and Animated peers will be that you are too negative, critical, and cold. And you are thinking, "Ha! They are illogical, irrational, and inconsistent!" Yes. They are not like you, and you are not like them. When we look through our own lenses, we can start to believe that our way is the best way and that everyone else is wrong. This is far from the truth. We need each other to make the world work; your team needs each person to accomplish the goal. You have your way, and your team members have theirs. When we can begin to appreciate each other's differences, we will reduce conflict and, ultimately, our stress.

Communicating with Other Styles

So, what is the best way to communicate with your peers, associates, friends, and family members who are not like you? Let's look at some strategies to help you build bridges and improve all your relationships.

Assertive Communicators

You and the Assertive communicator have something in common: you are both task oriented and want to get the job done. Because of this, you can communicate with Assertives with relatively little trouble. You simply need to stay focused on the facts and keep it businesslike. The one change you will want to incorporate is to avoid giving too much information on the front end. Remember, Accurate communicators are faster paced than you and are looking for the bottom line. These goal-oriented individuals are decisive, direct, and impatient.

A good approach with Assertive communicators is to prepare your message in advance. Focus on what is critical and important to Assertive communicators, and address it immediately. Once you have given the main focus, ask if they would like additional details. If they say yes, then proceed with your supporting data. If they say no, then let it go. No matter how hard you try, you will not get their attention. They will not listen to you. You will leave frustrated. Set yourself up for success by being a bit more direct with these folks, and all will go well.

Animated Communicators

Each personality has a complete opposite, and the Animated communicator is yours. They are faster paced than you, and they are more outgoing. They have a global outlook on things rather than concentrating on the nitty-gritty details. They can appear very disorganized to you. One of my clients, a very Accurate and Assertive person, gets very upset with Animated people because they seem to move very fast but never get anything done. This is a wrong assumption. Animated people are creative, and they are great at coaching others. Every team needs a cheerleader, so do not lessen the value of their contribution to the team by holding them to your standard.

When communicating with them, realize that they desire to enjoy the conversation and you! Be a bit more lively and informal in your discussions. Do not overload them with details but rather share experiences. Do not wait for your turn to jump in; you may wait a long time. You will need to merge into the conversation, especially if you have something important to say. They will not mind.

Attentive Communicators

Other slower paced individuals are the Attentive communicators. They lean more towards people than tasks, though. Since you share something with them, you can often communicate fairly easily with them. You both appreciate structure and a steady pace. Attentive communicators are much more sensitive than you, though. Be patient, warm, and kind with them as you share details.

Since they can be concerned about change, communicating the specifics to them will help them make transitions. Be personable and talk about nonwork things first to break the ice. Once they feel comfortable, you can move into the task at hand. I know that your mind goes straight to the facts, but if you can wait just a few minutes, some pleasantries will go a long way with these folks. You are not being manipulative or fake. You are striving to speak the right language for the right person. Keep that in mind, and you'll adjust to any situation or person with finesse and confidence.

Accurate Communicators

Your fellow Accurate communicators will be looking for concrete details, data, and specifics. This is all right up your alley! One caution is to not get stuck in the exchange. Remember, knowing and talking are not the same as taking action. Life revolves around the clock, schedules, and deadlines, so ensure that you both understand the time frame.

When you are communicating with others like you, you will find it effortless. You are both operating in your comfort zone. When you do that, it does not take energy. Adapting to the other styles will take some energy and effort. The good news is that you do not have to live there; you are simply visiting for a spell. And you will reap enormous benefits any time you build a bridge instead of a wall.

We Need Each Other

Take a moment to review the strengths and contributions that each communication style brings to the table. Write what you appreciate about them:

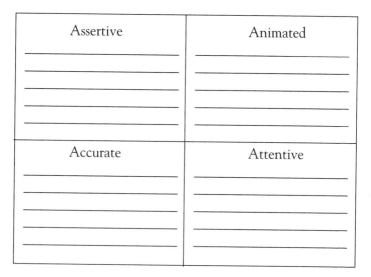

Assertive	Animated
Accurate	Attentive

Communication Cheat Sheet

Now, look at the people you work with specifically or those in your life. Look back at the descriptions (or chapters) of the different styles and begin to list each person's communication mode. This is not for judgmental purposes but for the sake of learning how best to talk, encourage, motivate, share, and speak to them. I know you want to respond correctly and properly to the different situations, and this can be your guide.

Communication Cheat Sheet				
Name	Key Words	Tone of Voice	Pace of Speech	Body Language
Person #1				
Person #2				
Person #3				
Person #4				
Person #5				

Keep practicing what you have learned about the four communication styles, and your life will become richer. No one is perfect, so if you do not do it just right, try, try again.

CHAPTER EIGHT

Presenting with Style

To be persuasive, we must be believable;
To be believable, we must be credible;
To be credible, we must be truthful.

Edward R. Murrow[1]

By this point in the book, you know the communication style of yourself and others in your life. We are hoping that you have learned to speak with Assertives about passion and the future, that you have encouraged the Animateds with fun and a focus on the team, that Attentives have been personally enriched by you, and that your Accurates have understood your structures, strategies, and systems. But working and communicating with people whom you know pretty well is very different from working and communicating with people you do not know and interact with on a regular basis. For instance, how can you leverage your communication style when you have to step up to the podium in a packed room or make a board presentation to people whom you don't know? How can you present with style in those environments? This chapter will help you leverage your communication style through effective presentations.

For some of us, speaking to small or large groups is no sweat. For others, making a presentation to a group is a terrible fate. In fact, many people rank their fear of public speaking as greater than their fear of death! Yikes. This brief chapter may not help you overcome your fear of speaking or make you an excellent speaker instantly (after all, you know that "Rome was not built in a day"); however, I (John) have learned over time that if you can answer a few critical questions, you are well on your way to giving presentations with style. The key to great presentations lies in answering these questions:

Who am I?
What am I presenting?
To whom am I presenting?

Who Am I?

You may feel that you cannot control this, especially in a corporate setting. But you have to. Everything you present has to flow organically and authentically from who you are. You will not, over time, make presentations with style if the content of the presentation does not connect with *who* you are and what you are passionate about. In chapter 10, Lorraine will talk about "selling with style." But for now, accept this maxim: whenever you make a presentation, you *are* selling yourself. Spend a few moments and think through these key questions:

1. What are the core values of your life? What do you so highly value that, if your job required you to transgress those values and beliefs, you would be willing to quit your job? If you could afford to, what activities in your life would you do for the rest of your life without pay?

_____

_____

_____

_____

_____

_____

2. What makes you laugh? What makes you dance? What makes you cry? What makes you sing?

_____

_____

_____

_____

_____

_____

3. Think ahead five years. What achievement, relationship, status, circumstance, or experience would bring peace and contentment into your life if you had arrived at that place?

_____

_____

_____

_____

_____

As you think through these questions, find the key elements of your presentation(s) that link with your core values, passion, and dreams. Knowing *who* you are and what your core values, passions, and dreams are will help you leverage your presentation style.

What Am I Presenting?

Knowing who you are gets you "suited up" for the game. Knowing *what* you are going to speak about means that you understand the game you are playing. Guy Kawasaki, serial entrepreneur of Apple Computer and famous for venture capital funding, says in his blog that there are many specific ways to get a standing ovation as a speaker. Here are four key points from that blog entry[2] that I've modified for our purposes:

- **Have something interesting to say.** If I am in the audience, I have to know if this is worth my time. Do not waste my time telling me something that you are not interested in or passionate about.
- **Cut the sales pitch.** Do not sell me; entertain me. If I like *you*, then I will be far more open to your presentation. See the book *The Likeability Factor* by Tim Sanders regarding this point.
- **Know your audience.** Walk around before your presentation. Study your audience before you meet with them and know what they are all about. (I'll be addressing this a little bit later.)
- **Tell stories.** Good ones. Ideally, your story should support your presentation focus.

How well do you know your presentation? What are the key benefits you will share with your audience? How do those benefits specifically meet needs that might be present in your audience? Do everything possible to internalize your presentation. Since I speak every single week in front of multiple sized audiences, you would think that I would have long ago conquered my nervousness. Not so! Every week I go over my notes *multiple* times before a presentation as part of the process of internalizing what I am going to communicate.

The Perfect Example

Without a doubt, Jesus Christ was the greatest speaker ever. Here is just one account of audience response from his time:

"When Jesus had finished saying these things, the crowds were amazed at his teaching, because he taught as one who had authority, and not as their teachers of the law" (Matthew 7:28-29 NIV). (You can also find similar reactions in the Bible at Matthew 22:33 and Mark 11:18 and 12:37.) The following are some suggestions from the teaching of Jesus.

Think about how your presentation could be described in these terms. Jesus started his talks with consideration of people's hurts, needs, and interests. How about your presentation? What are the needs of your audience?

People seemed to enjoy Jesus' speaking to them (see the verses listed above). Is there anything about your presentation that is particularly interesting, intriguing, humorous, or unique?

Make a list of the characteristics of your presentation. After you list these characteristics, think of ways that you can make what you say "stick" for your audiences. Is your presentation:

Memorable? _____

Unique? _____

Interesting? _____

Beneficial? _____

To Whom Am I Presenting?

The more you know about your audience, the more likely it is that your presentation will be able to connect your passions, values, and dreams to your audience's needs, interests, and desires. By utilizing what you have learned already in *Leveraging Your Communication Style*, you know that members of each style will be represented in your audience. So, what do they need to hear?

Assertives will need to hear about passion and future. You will have to emphasize the ability of your product to bring about positive change and to enhance the future in order to capture the heart of the Assertive. You can do this! When you link your values, passions, and dreams with the capabilities of your product, you will be able to connect to the heart and mind of the Assertives in your audience.

What about your presentation will be most appealing to Assertives?

Animateds want to know how your product will help them help their team. What is it about your product or presentation that will enhance the environment and experience of their team? If you can link your personal story to a greater team theme and then provide the link between your story and your product, you will have the listening ear of the Animateds in your audience. Remember that Animateds will be looking for the *energy* in your presentation, so be sure to engage that portion of your audience with hand and facial gestures.

What about your presentation will be most appealing to Animateds?

Attentives want to hear that your product will change the life experience of the people they know and love. So, has your product changed *your* life? Does it enhance the quality and focus of your life? As an Attentive, I want to know that you *believe* in what you are saying and presenting to me. If you can show that you have personally benefited and that your product or service will benefit the lives of others in a personal and fulfilling fashion, you'll have Attentives ready to respond to you.

What about your presentation will be most appealing to Attentives?

_____

_____

_____

_____

Accurates want to know that the systems and strategies of their lives are efficient and effective. You will not stand a chance presenting with style to Accurates unless you can convince them that you have done your homework and your details are correct and precise. Once you have done your homework, if you convince Accurates that your product will increase efficiency and effectiveness for them and those they influence, then you will have them on your team.

So, what about your presentation will help Accurates achieve maximum efficiency at a personal and team level? What about your presentation will be most appealing to Accurates?

_____

_____

_____

_____

Putting It All Together

When you make a presentation, you are speaking to a crowd. The "room" itself will hear you, so you should know yourself, what you are speaking about, and to whom you are speaking to the best of your ability. But at the end of the day, presenting with style is just like all good communication and leadership—it is leveraging your influence in the context of positive and proactive relationships. So you are not just presenting to the room; you are presenting to Assertives who dream of building a healthy future, Animateds who dream of building a healthy team, Attentives who dream of helping build healthy individuals, and Accurates who want to build a healthy system. So go ahead and present to them—with style!

CHAPTER NINE

Managing and Reducing Conflict with Style

When we understand ourselves and others, we are able to communicate more effectively, enjoy better relationships, and create more effective teams.

Steven R. Smith[1]

When I (John) was in my mid-twenties, I was at a particularly stress-filled time of life. The details are not that important, but they included the realities of completing a doctorate at a major university, being a new parent, and having a full-time, intense, conflict-oriented job. During one horrible time of that period of life, I broke out in a skin rash over most of my upper body. I went to a doctor who examined me fairly thoroughly. Then he gave me his diagnosis and prescription: "You have a stress-induced rash. This rash is how your body is telling you that you are 'red-lining' with stress. I recommend that you eliminate stress from your life." I laughed out loud! I said, "Doctor, do you have any stress in your life?" Then he laughed out loud! After a brief conversation, I think we came to an agreement. The goal was *reducing and managing* stress, not eliminating it. Stress is actually a good thing and can be quite energizing and life-giving as long as it is managed in a healthy fashion.

You are a person of influence. You influence others through positive and proactive communication in the context of healthy relationships. So conflict is not part of your life, right? *Wrong!* Conflict, like stress, is an inevitable reality of human life and particularly in the context of relationships. Regardless of what your communication style is, you *will* experience conflict with your team members, family members, and friends. The goal is not to eliminate conflict, but to manage it in a way that sustains healthy relationships. I want to equip you to manage conflict with style, but in order to do that, we need to become familiar with some destructive patterns of conflict.

Destructive Conflict Patterns

Here are five different descriptions of destructive conflict patterns. As you read them, think about the family you grew up in, the marriage you are in, or a relational conflict you have experienced. Do you see any patterns that typify the way that you or those close to you handle conflict?

The first kind is the *Eskimo*. This is when you are in the middle of a conflict and you just freeze people out. You just shut down and have what I call a "cold war." You say, "Okay, we are in conflict, I will not communicate; I am shutting down, and you are getting the ice treatment." This is a very destructive way to go about conflict.

A second style is known as the *Cowboy*. The cowboy basically takes the six-shooters and says, "Okay, you want to fight, let's go—boom, boom, boom" and sends a barrage of verbal bullets that tear apart the recipient. This is a very destructive way to have conflict.

The third way is the *Genie* in a bottle. You know what a genie in a bottle is? Basically in the middle of conflict that is the person who says, "Look, you say I am a dummy? I'm a dummy. You say that I need to do this? I'll do that." This is the person who is compliant, who does whatever you want in order to get out of the conflict but never really resolves the issue.

The fourth kind of destructive conflict style is known as the *Houdini*. This is the person who says, "I'm out of here. If we're having conflict, I am gone; I am out the door; I'm out of the room; I'm just not going to be anywhere near conflict."

The fifth kind of conflict style is the *Attila the Hun*. This is the kind of person who goes for the jugular and is very destructive. In fact, some of you understand that you can actually go over the line here. This is a person who becomes enraged and is not only verbally and emotionally, but sometimes even physically, destructive.

All of these are negative and destructive patterns of conflict. We must learn to control our anger and, in doing that, be able to build up relationships, not tear them down. As someone who has been involved in managing conflict among

99

teams that work together closely over periods of years, I have learned a number of tools that help ensure healthy relationships. Here is a brief list of some "Dos and Don'ts" that will help you manage conflict with style:

DON'T	DO
Assume	Ask questions
Focus on the negative	Concentrate on the positive
Listen to the words	Hear what they are saying
Be passive or aggressive	Be assertive
Use "You" statements	Use "I" statements
Bring up past issues	Focus on the issues at hand
Concentrate on the person	Concentrate on the issue
Blame others	Accept blame
Try to win	Go for the win-win!

Here is the truth: All people—even people with long fuses—face conflict in their relationships. And in the absence of conscious training in healthy ways to deal with the anger that arises, most people will approach conflict in the way most familiar to them. In their book *Fit to Be Tied*, Bill and Lynne Hybels observe:

> Because they have not been coached or trained, they will have no emergency procedures to fall back on. So what will they do? In most cases, they will resort to the only conflict resolution procedures they are familiar with: the ones their parents used. Even if they witnessed an unhealthy, unacceptable method of conflict resolution,

and even if they vowed they would never behave that way, in the absence of proper training, they will almost inevitably revert to the method they grew up with.[2]

Have you ever noticed yourself in the middle of a disagreement sounding just like your mother? Or acting suspiciously like your dad? It happens all the time. Each one of us needs to recognize our conflict style right along with our communication style. Any of the five conflict styles above can be destructive and unhealthy. Here are my two key suggestions for managing conflict with style in order to ensure that the relationships on your team and in your life stay healthy:

1. When a relationship is broken, take responsibility for seeking reconciliation. In other words, you need to be the one to initiate the repair of the relationship. I know, it cuts against the grain of our society and perhaps our own experience and personality. But unresolved conflict is a recipe for disaster and destruction. In fact, I personally believe that unresolved conflict is like cancer—malignant, fast growing, and always destructive. Do not delay; just do it!

2. Be willing to say the hard things. In other words, if you have difficult things to speak about, do it carefully. Think through the other person's communication style before you approach that person, but do it. Sometimes on our team (borrowing a phrase we heard somewhere else), we say, "Be willing to say the last 10 percent."

Because we fear facing the consequences of dealing with hard stuff, we will sometimes avoid the "last 10 percent," which is the most difficult. It is our experience that the last 10 percent is the critical piece. Leaving it unresolved leaves everyone poorer. Unresolved conflict and a lack of authenticity and integrity in relationships are guaranteed to poison the environment of your team. My favorite resource in this regard is Patrick Lencioni's book, *Five Dysfunctions of a Team*. I think Patrick has done a marvelous job in providing tools for understanding that a healthy team operates with trust and that healthy conflict is the foundation for high performance.

On my primary team at work, I am privileged to serve with several team members whom I have known over the course of two decades. People looking in from the outside might assume that we are "conflict free." Boy, would they be wrong! We have had lots of conflict over the years. However, to the great credit of these team members, we have learned that conflict is a necessary and essential part of life. Handling our conflict quickly, clearly, and truthfully is important to us, and when we handle our conflict well, our team becomes stronger because of it. We like the old saying, "What doesn't kill you will make you stronger!"

Each communication style also tends to have a "conflict" style that is attached to it, so each of us has to watch not only our pattern of conflict but also how our personality style intersects with our conflict style. Here is a quick "primer" on that subject to assist you:

- If you are an Assertive, you probably tend to engage in conflict fairly quickly (and often!) because you see it as necessary to engage the future. Be careful about that tendency because conflict can sometimes destroy the relational fabric that other styles depend upon for health.

- If you are an Animated, you enjoy conversation and group process, so you will probably be pretty quick to "mix it up" with others during a conflict time. Just remember that the nursery rhyme, "Sticks and stones may break my bones, but words will never hurt me" is *wrong!* Words can bring real damage into the soul of someone, so you will have to watch how you use your words. Remember, words are like a tube of toothpaste—they come out easily, but try putting them back in the tube!

- If you are an Attentive, you value how others are thinking and feeling so much that you will most likely try to avoid conflict in order to eliminate pain. Remember, the goal is not to eliminate stress but to manage and reduce it, so engage in conflict carefully, always with an eye toward relational health.

- If you are an Accurate, then sometimes in order to protect the relational fabric of a team, you have to be willing to let go of a contentious issue. As an Accurate, you know that you have thought about the "best" way to do something. However, sometimes when we are so focused on the best way, we end up in "win-lose" kinds of arguments. It might be better on occasion to let go of something in order to arrive at win-win. Enter conflict carefully, and do not always fight to the death! Better to be happy than right.

Managing conflict with style is all about replacing unhealthy conflict patterns that you might have learned from your early life experiences with healthy patterns of relational life. Learn that, instead of fueling or fearing conflict, you can manage conflict in a healthy way by facing it with integrity. You will do that as you consider the other person's communication style and speak to him or her in a way that values that person, speaks the truth, and aims for a healthy relationship outcome where trust is increased and respect is maintained. When you manage conflict in a healthy way, your relationship with your team members will actually improve!

CHAPTER TEN

Selling with Style

---

*To get others to do what you want them to do, you must see
things through their eyes.*

David J. Schwartz[1]

No matter what your title or what you do, you are selling
something . . . even if it is only you and your ideas. Sales
is nothing more than relationship building, and all relationships require communication. In my (Lorraine's) opinion, the
golden rule of sales is that the relationship should come first.
As a business consultant, one of the many hats I have worn is
that of Key Account Sales Representative. I have been hired
to meet with major accounts and to sell books, videos, and
other products into large distribution channels. One of the
reasons that these national accounts have worked with me
over the years and why I was able to get results for my clients
was that I always put the relationship first. If a product was
not a good fit, I would tell the distributors up front. I did not
want them to be disappointed. If it would not sell for them, no
one would win in the long run. So when I did tell them something was a fit, they believed me, and I would get a large order.

Thinking Long-term

I think many sales people get caught up in the moment as they strive for a certain goal or bonus. But we must think long-term with people, not just the sale of the day. When people know that they matter to you, you can achieve great things together. Why? Because a strong foundation is build upon trust. You have heard the saying, "Trust is easily broken and difficult to regain." Good salespeople have trust and rapport with people.

Understanding the unique personality of those you are selling to can help you speak their language, thus building trust and rapport. And it will increase your sales close ratio! Who does not want that?

Closing the Sale at Hello!

Below is a chart with characteristics of the different communication styles and how you can adapt to sell to each style. When I am going out on a sales call to an Accurate communicator, I come prepared with all the details required to speak with a person with this communication style. Remember, he or she will want to review and consider your proposition before making a decision. If I find I have an Assertive communicator, I put the details aside and go straight for the bottom line. I go straight to it with no delay. If I am meeting with an Animated communicator, I show more of the pictures and engage in social conversation. I will not jump right into business, which is the same for an Attentive communicator. However, with Attentives, I keep the tone a little softer and slower, more personal. Take a look at the chart, and I'll have some additional tips and suggestions for you after it.

STYLE	ASSERTIVE	ANIMATED	ATTENTIVE	ACCURATE
Emphasize:	Opportunities/Results	People/Fun	Support/Service	Facts/Quality
Act:	Direct and Businesslike	Friendly and Upbeat	Personable and Authentic	Logical and Consistent
Key to Success: Answer This Question	*What* is in it for them?	*Who* is using your product or service?	*Why* is your product or service right for them?	*How* will your product make things better or more efficient?
Do . . .	Focus on the bottom line.	Show them how they can engage with your product or service.	Ensure reliability and dependability.	Give them time to analyze and process.
Don't . . .	Tell them what to do!	Give too many details.	Be pushy or aggressive.	Be demanding or disorganized.
Expect Them to Be:	Fast-paced, Impatient	Fast-paced, Disorganized	Slower-paced, Indecisive	Slower-paced, Inflexible

STYLE	ASSERTIVE	ANIMATED	ATTENTIVE	ACCURATE
Visual/Voice Cues:	Sharp Clothes, Professional, Expensive Jewelry, Direct	Trendy Clothes, Friendly, Lots of Jewelry, Talkative	Soft Clothes, Warm, Minimal Jewelry, Quiet	Practical Clothes, Cold, Glasses, Cautious
Office Décor:	Clean, "Power" Colors, Professional, Some Order	Bright/Colorful, Photos of People, Cluttered Desk, Office Awards	Many Family Photos, "Cozy" Feeling, Some Clutter	Very Clean, Organized, Minimal Distractions
Hand Shake:	Firm, Roll over to Top	Energetic, Big Movements	Gentle, Submissive	Correct for the Situation

What I love about this is that you can actually, *visually*, see whom you are dealing with immediately and make adjustments accordingly. Recently, I was in the airport waiting for a very early morning flight and saw this bright lime green with hot pink accents outfit standing over to the side. It was so bright it was hurting my eyes. As I looked over my shoulder, I saw a famous singer. She is Animated for sure and proud of it! Start paying attention to those around you. Notice what they are wearing, how much jewelry, the pace of their walk, and so on. For those who may do most of their work on the phone, you are in luck. You can identify someone's communication style within minutes on the telephone. Simply listen to that person's tone (is it direct, bubbly, gentle, or restrained?), notice the pace (fast or slow), and react as necessary. If that person appears impatient, pick up the pace! If he or she is expressing things in specific details, provide a lot of facts.

Learning to recognize these cues will not only help you understand and communicate better with others, it will pay off in sales! One of my clients had me present a *Selling with Style* program to his seasoned sales staff. Some of his sales associates were having difficulty with their accounts and needed something that would take them beyond traditional selling techniques, which they already knew quite well. I gave them these tips and suggestions for noting the communication styles of their potential buyers, and it worked! My client told me that in the weeks and months after my presentation, his sales associates worked to tailor their approach to each particular contact and ended up closing deals in less time. "Bottom line: it got us results!" he said.

Successful Communication

Anyone who wants to be effective in any arena of life, and particularly in communication, will be forever working on his or her craft. Communication is an art, not a science. Effective communicators are consistently aware of two primary realities: (1) Who am I as a person and communicator? and (2) To whom am I speaking, and what is their perspective? Regardless of whether you are trying to persuade or inform, your communication skills will increase over time as you learn to practice effective communication with persistence. Salespeople have discovered this as well, recognizing that selling, relationships, and persistency all go hand in hand! A survey by a national sales association found:

48 percent of all salespersons make one call, then cross off the prospect.
25 percent quit after the second call.
12 percent call three times and then quit.
10 percent keep calling.
80 percent of all new sales are made after the fifth call to the same prospect.[2]

So, you want to be a better communicator? Keep on pursuing those relationships! The more you communicate and develop relationships with people of other communication styles, the better a communicator you will become!

You Make the Call

Let's go ahead and practice applying some of these techniques. Read the situational questions and answer them to the best of your ability. I'll provide help and thoughts at the end.

1. If you walked into an office and saw a bunch of awards on the wall, plaques and trophies, with whom might you be meeting? How would you communicate with them?

_____

_____

_____

_____

2. If you made a cold call and the person on the other end of the phone was impatient, direct, and a bit forceful—wanting to know why you called—how could you get his or her attention and pitch your product or service?

_____

_____

_____

_____

3. During a trade show, a potential customer is reading every piece of literature you have and examining your product closely. What would be the best approach to them?

_____

_____

_____

_____

_____

4. A customer walks into your office wearing soft, comfortable clothes with minimal jewelry and quietly greets you. Whom might you be dealing with, and how should you begin the sales call?

_____

_____

_____

_____

_____

The Outcome

Now, we are making generalizations here that do not include one's upbringing, spiritual life, or any other factors that can influence who they are, but I have to tell you that these visual and behavioral cues really work! If you determined that the first potential client was most likely an Animated communicator, you were correct! You would want to be very social and get them talking, probably about himself or herself! Get the energy going, and you will have a fan. Then, selling your product or service will be a slam-dunk.

For the second scenario, if you felt you had an Assertive communicator on the line, you pegged it. You would need to get straight to the bottom line of what you, your product, or your service could do for that person, like save a lot of money. Once the Assertive communicator sees the benefit, allow him or her to ask questions. Do not give too much detail, only as it is requested. And never, ever tell this person what to do. These folks need to be in the driver's seat.

For the third case, you probably guessed that you had an Accurate communicator on your hands. Right again! The best approach for this person would be to give a bag with every brochure you have along with endorsements, samples, and so on. Encourage the Accurate communicator to review it at leisure. Get this person's business card and set a date to follow up . . . and keep it! I know you have heard that if a customer walks away, you have reduced your chances of success. This is not the case with Accurate communicators. If you push this type too fast, you will get an answer, but the answer will be *no!* Work with his or her timetable, and you will win a faithful customer.

The last scenario portrayed an Attentive communicator. You would want to get to know each other on a personal basis first. Talk about your family and maybe what that person likes to do. Then when he or she is feeling comfortable, start talking business. Ask questions to pull the Attentive communicator in, but give him or her enough time to answer them. Do not be too forceful or direct, but you can suggest a purchase. If this person trusts you, he or she will buy.

Selling with Style!

Some people might think that adapting one's self to another style is fake and manipulative. I do not feel that this is the case; in fact, I believe it is respectful to speak to a person's style. My husband and I travel to Mexico occasionally, and we attempt to speak Spanish when we are in the country. Now, our Spanish is not very good, but we try. The locals always appreciate our efforts and help us along. They feel respected. Sales is no different. If we come into situations and expect others to work with *who* we are, then we have a barrier between us. We have just made the sale more difficult to make because we first must scale the wall that is between us. Once we are over, we can then talk about the product or service. By building a bridge and speaking the customer's language, on the other hand, you can go right into the business at hand. You do not have obstacles to overcome. You have created a foundation of trust, and it all begins with trust.

When I was looking for a new car a few years back, I told the salesman that I had something very specific in mind and provided the details: sporty, black, sun roof, and the price range. I said I was ready to buy and wanted to see what he had that matched my profile. He proceeded to walk me by every single car on the lot, and he told me the most intricate details of how *every* car was made, down to every nut and bolt! I tried to be gracious, but after about thirty minutes, I walked away. I could not get a word in edgewise because he had his "script" of trying to sell the product based upon how it was built. I did not care! I just wanted some wheels within my criteria. He lost the sale! The worst part is that he probably thought I did not like the cars; in reality, I did not like his approach. He did not read my body language, nor did he give me an opportunity to tell him that I was not interested in the facts but on making a decision. He spoke his Accurate language to an Assertive communicator. He bombed.

I encourage you to use the chart and apply it to phone calls, sales calls, trade shows, and even the workplace. We are always selling something: ideas, visions, opinions, products, services, and so on. Why not do it with style and see better results?

Here's a saying I came up with as a reminder for working on our communication with clients:

Send them home happy.
Engage them.

Remind them that you appreciate their business.
View complaints as an opportunity to improve.
Interact with them often.
Care for their needs.
End each experience on a positive note.

CONCLUSION

Leveraging Your Communication Style

We cannot become what we need to be by remaining what we are.

Max De Pree[1]

I (John) speak every week to large audiences. That part of my life might seem very different from yours. I assure you that I struggle with it every week; however, I also work every week with a team of colleagues with very different traits and styles. I sometimes get frustrated with them, and they get frustrated with me (more than I'd ever like to admit!). Periodically I'll let myself go on this line of thinking: *My team members don't get it. If they would just see things like I see them and understand things like I understand them, it would be so much easier. If only they would communicate to me like I want them to, it would all be "peaches and cream."* But then, when I am thinking like that, I stop myself pretty quickly. What a horrible world that would be! The world does not need more of me. In fact, I deeply need people like my team members around me. Truthfully, it is *because* they are different from me that we make a good team. Healthy teams are made up of contributing members who complement and complete each other. Harvey Mackay says in his book *Dig Your Well Before You're Thirsty* that "your network (team) should not look just like you. If it does, you have an anthill, not a network."[2] I want to be on the team that wins because each member played his or her part and we accomplished the goal.

You may never end up speaking before large audiences. Communicating with large groups or making formal presentations to boards or organizations may never be your forte. We think this book will help you be more effective in these arenas; however, every one of us communicates with others. You have people in your life right now who need what you have. They are waiting for you to contribute what you have to the team. Both Lorraine and I believe in you. You are a person of influence. You can increase your influence by leveraging your communication style. It is our hope that this book moved you substantially forward in that goal by equipping you to understand yourself and others whom you work with on a regular basis.

So now what? Throughout this book, we have given you tools to increase your self-understanding and your awareness of the communication styles of those around you. How you move to the next level of communication effectiveness is up to you. If you take responsibility for this area of your life, we are sure that your influence will increase. Begin by being clear about who you are; move ahead by becoming clear about who others are; complete the journey by communicating with style to those on your team and in your life and by making effective communication a priority for your whole team.

Positive and proactive influence in the context of healthy relationships means that you will recognize the critical role that communication plays in relationships. When I occasionally do marriage counseling, it is amazing how many issues ultimately come back to communication. Money, goals, intimacy, responsibilities, emotions, and life experience all are well-traveled roads paved with the "asphalt" of communication. By reading and exploring this book, you have demonstrated your willingness to engage in a foundational subject for all areas of life!

On a more personal note, I would like to tell you that communicating with people as individuals is something that I have had to practice and develop over years. When I was in my early adolescence, I learned that I could communicate well to groups. So what makes most people terrified (public speaking before groups) comes rather "naturally" to me. I now speak in front of audiences of varying sizes on a regular basis. But you know what can cause me substantial discomfort? Communicating with people who may not know my heart and whose heart I may not know. So I wrote this book with Lorraine in part to make sure that I committed to leveraging my communication style with those I love and work with each week. I hope you have grown through what you have learned in this book. I know I have. Thanks for taking the journey with us!

Dr. John Jackson

Besides being a writer, I (Lorraine) am also a fitness trainer and instructor, and I see plenty of people avoiding exercise at any cost. Communication, however, is something no one can avoid; communication is mandatory for life here on earth. Even when you are not saying something, you are communicating! Ever have someone stare at you? That person is telling you something without opening his or her mouth.

The invention of technology was supposed to make our lives easier, but the reality is that it has hindered our ability to communicate verbally with one another. An entire generation has learned how to interact and socialize with technology, not necessarily in person. E-mail and text messages often have shortcuts like using all caps that can offend recipients. When I read about the man who broke up with his fiancé via e-mail, I decided that we are sliding down a slippery slope. We are becoming controlled by technology rather than controlling it. Technology should serve us, not be a means to do and say things we could not or would not say in person. And we wonder why conflict abounds everywhere we turn.

I do not know how the rest of the country is doing, but I do see more conflict here in California. Over the short five years I have lived in my community, I have seen more and more people verbally attacking each other in parking lots—over a parking space! I hear more honking and see more inappropriate gestures from drivers. Even in the stores, people are ramming into each other's carts to get ahead of them in line. We are losing our common courtesies (which is another book for another day), but we also seem to be communicating poorly with each other.

Most people do not understand the different communication styles and are at a disadvantage. You are ahead of the curve now that you have read *Leveraging Your Communication Style*. You now have the ability to identify a person's communication style, and you have the tools to adapt your message to meet that person's needs. But, as with anything, you must take the knowledge from the book and put it into practice in your life. The world needs you! By being an example of better communication, you can start a trend. People will often react as they are treated. Use the graphs and charts to assist you in understanding the other styles. The more you practice, the easier it will become to transition smoothly from one approach to another. It is amazing when it is in action! People will react positively and enjoy your company more. Previously strained relationships can be mended, and all relationships can be made stronger.

At the conclusion of one of my *Communicating with Style* two-day seminars, a lady came up crying. Once she gained her composure, she said that she had called her estranged sister the night before. They had not spoken in twenty years. She shared with her sister how she had learned that they were very different styles. She was an Attentive communicator, and her sister was an Assertive communicator. They had had nothing but conflict and frustration throughout their lives and finally decided not to speak. This woman took a brave and bold step; she apologized to her sister and said that she had expected her sister to be just like she herself was. Because her sister was not, this woman had become hurt and upset. She now realized that her sister was just being who she was, not doing anything on purpose to harm her. They reconciled. That is the power in this information.

On the job front, you will be a living example of great leadership by the way you effectively communicate in myriad circumstances. Nothing will stump you, and you will work well with *all* team members. So rather than resisting minor changes you can make, I encourage you to embrace them. Make them your own.

Throughout this book, we have given support as to why this method works and detailed ways you can use it with your communication. In case you still need some motivation to incorporate this into your life, here are some additional benefits you stand to gain, based on your unique communication style:

Assertive	Animated
• Sell your ideas faster • Get solid buy-in on visions • Negotiate successfully • Spend less time struggling and more time on the issues at hand	• Enjoy relationships more • Improve friendships at work and home • Reduce stressful, awkward, or embarrassing situations

Accurate	Attentive
• Say the right thing at the right time in the right way • Discuss important issues in a correct manner • Communicate effectively and efficiently	• Support and care for people for who they are • Build deeper and stronger relationships • Avoid conflict and reduce stress

Others may not always appreciate your efforts to understand and work with them in their own styles, but as I often remind myself, "Be Generous."

Be generous
with your time and give it away.
Make sure you do it each and every day.

Be generous
with thoughtful words you speak.
Make sure it is kindness that you seek.

Be generous
with your love, compassion and your deeds.
Remember you are planting hopeful seeds.

Be generous
  with your prayers for mercy and grace.
  And always keep your eyes upon His heavenly face.

Be generous
  with material items you have obtained
  and words of the One who helped you gain.

Be generous
  with your entire life.
  It's way too short to have any strife.

Be generous.

Remember that every little step you take will get you closer to communicating with style. May you have enhanced relationships, build more bridges than walls, and experience less conflict and more happiness. God bless you!

Lorraine Bossé-Smith

Notes

1. The Fine Art of Communication

1. Quoted in Glenn van Ekern, *The Speaker's Sourcebook II* (Englewood Cliffs, N.J.: Prentice Hall, 1994), 70.

2. The Churchill Centre, "Speeches and Quotations," http://www.winstonchurchill.org/i4a/pages/index.cfm?pageid=388 (accessed November 29, 2007).

3. Boyd Clarke and Ron Crossland, *The Leader's Voice: How Your Communication Can Inspire Action and Get Results!* (New York: Select Books, 2002); see also http://hbswk.hbs.edu/archive/3559.html (accessed August 30, 2007).

4. Michael Quicke, *360-Degree Preaching* (Grand Rapids, Mich.: Baker Academic, 2003), 14.

2. Discovering Your Communication Style

1. Quoted in Glenn van Ekern, *The Speaker's Sourcebook II* (Englewood Cliffs, N.J.: Prentice Hall, 1994), 283.

2. Joe Jones, "You Talk Too Much," words and music by Reginald Hall and Joe Jones, © EMI Longitude Music.

3. Alan Chapman, "Personality Theories, Types, and Tests,"

http://www.businessballs.com/personalitystylesmodels.htm (accessed August 21, 2007), 4.

3. Understanding Your Communication Style

1. Quoted in Glenn van Ekern, *The Speaker's Sourcebook II* (Englewood Cliffs, N.J.: Prentice Hall, 1994), 360.

4. Assertive Communicators

1. Quoted in Dennis W. Bakke, *Joy At Work* (Seattle: P V G), 134.

5. Animated Communicators

1. Quoted in Glenn van Ekern, *The Speaker's Sourcebook II* (Englewood Cliffs, N.J.: Prentice Hall, 1994), 318.

2. © Ralston Purina Company, 2002.

6. Attentive Communicators

1. Quoted in Glenn van Ekern, *The Speaker's Sourcebook II* (Englewood Cliffs, N.J.: Prentice Hall, 1994), 317.

7. Accurate Communicators

1. Mark H. McCormack, *What They Don't Teach You in Harvard Business School* (New York: Bantam Books, 1984), 237.

2. Data from *InSight*, Syncrude Canada Ltd., Communications Division.

8. Presenting with Style

1. Quoted in Glenn van Ekern, *The Speaker's Sourcebook II* (Englewood Cliffs, N.J.: Prentice Hall, 1994), 288.

2. Guy Kawasaki, "How to Get a Standing Ovation," *How to Change the World*, http://blog.guykawasaki.com/2006/01/how_to_get_a_st.html (accessed May 20, 2008).

9. Managing and Reducing Conflict with Style

1. Quoted in Steven R. Smith, *Mastering Communication Workbook* (Murrieta, Calif.: Concept One, 2002), 5.

2. Bill and Lynne Hybels, *Fit to Be Tied* (Grand Rapids, Mich.: Zondervan, 1991), 120.

10. Selling with Style

1. Quoted in Glenn van Ekern, *The Speaker's Sourcebook II* (Englewood Cliffs, N.J.: Prentice Hall, 1994), 288.

2. John Maxwell, *The Success Journey* (Nashville: Thomas Nelson, 1997), 137.

Conclusion: Leveraging Your Communication Style

1. Quoted in Glenn van Ekern, *The Speaker's Sourcebook II* (Englewood Cliffs, N.J.: Prentice Hall, 1994), 179.

2. Harvey Mckay, *Dig Your Well Before You're Thirsty* (New York: Doubleday, 1997).

Bibliography

Bakke, Raymond. *Joy at Work*. Seattle: PVG, 2005.

Chapman, Alan. "Personality Theories, Types, and Tests." *Business Balls*. http://www.businessballs.com/personalitystylesmodels.htm.

Clarke, Boyd, and Ron Crossland. *The Leader's Voice: How Your Communication Can Inspire Action and Get Results*. New York: Select Books, 2002.

Covey, Stephen. *Seven Habits of Highly Effective People*. New York: Simon & Schuster, 1989.

Hybels, Bill, and Lynne Hybels. *Fit to Be Tied*. Grand Rapids, Mich.: Zondervan, 1991.

Kawasaki, Guy. "How to Get a Standing Ovation." *How to Change the World*. http://blog.guykawasaki.com/2006/01/how_to_get_a_st. html.

Lencioni, Patrick. *Five Dysfunctions of a Team*. San Francisco: Jossey Bass, 2002.

Mackay, Harvey. *Dig Your Well Before You're Thirsty*. New York: Doubleday, 1997.

Maxwell, John. *The Leadership Bible, NIV*. Grand Rapids, Mich.: Zondervan, 1998.

———. *The Success Journey*. Nashville: Thomas Nelson, 1997.

McCormack, Mark H. *What They Don't Teach You in Harvard Business School*. New York: Bantam Books, 1984.

Online Women's Business Center. "Understanding Your Communication Style." *Air War College Communication Skills.* http://www.au.af.mil /au/awc/awcgate/sba/comm_style.htm.

Quicke, Michael. *360-Degree Preaching.* Grand Rapids, Mich.: Baker Academic, 2003.

Smith, Steven R. *Mastering Communication Workbook.* Murrieta, Calif.: Concept One, 2002.

van Ekern, Glenn. *The Speaker's Sourcebook II.* Englewood Cliffs, N.J.: Prentice Hall, 1994.